International
Medical Communication
in English

International Medical Communication in English

John Christopher Maher

English for Special Purposes
John Swales, editor

Ann Arbor
THE UNIVERSITY OF MICHIGAN PRESS

Library of Congress Cataloging-in-Publication Data

Maher, John Christopher.
   International medical communication in English / John Christopher
Maher.
      p.   cm. — (English for special purposes)
   Originally published: Edinburgh : Edinburgh University Press,
1990.
    ISBN 0-472-08174-8 (alk. paper)
   1. English language—Medical English.   2. English language—Study
and teaching—Foreign speakers.   I. Title.   II. Series.
    [DNLM: 1. Communication.   2. Physician-Patient Relations.
3. Writing.   WZ 345 M214i]
R118.M34   1992
428.2'4'002461—dc20
DNLM/DLC
for Library of Congress   91-36916
                                   CIP

Contents

Preface

This reference manual is designed to meet the international communication needs of medical professionals of all levels whose first language is not English. Essentially a medical English "Do-It-Yourself" book, it provides guidance on a range of communication skills, such as telephoning in a hospital and how to present papers at medical meetings, write letters, and write papers for medical journals. Those who may find the book useful are doctors, medical students, dentists, nurses, and medical researchers.

Most users of this handbook will have some knowledge of English, but may still need help in communicating successfully in a variety of medical situations. This is not an exercise book. Many medical textbooks are already available. This reference book is a multi-skill handbook that provides models of effective communication in:

Presenting papers at medical meetings/conferences
Techniques of discussion at medical meetings
Writing medical reports and journal articles
Everyday language of doctor-patient communication
Understanding medical terminology
Telephoning in a hospital.

This handbook also includes reference sections on medical abbreviations, a medical vocabulary "test section," language functions for use in medical writing, medical terminology, labeling of medical instruments and equipment, and PLAB/FMG and language test information.

On the question of "style" (British or American) this book adopts a global perspective. I have strenuously avoided a narrow, culture-bound approach as far as possible. Medical people around the world are generally unconcerned as to which "model" is used so long as the communication is appropriate and effective. I have been conscious throughout the preparation of this book that it is intended for doctors and medical professionals around the world in countries where English may not be a first language (as well as in North America, Britain, Australia, etc.). Because of its comprehensive coverage and explanations this handbook can be used for self-study as well as for selected purposes in class.

Tokyo, 1989   J.C.M.

Acknowledgments

There are many people who have helped in the preparation of this book. It would be impossible to thank them all but I would like to thank those people in particular whose wisdom, advice and encouragement have made this book possible: Shoso Yamamoto M.D., Bernard Naylor M.D., Chuzo Mori M.D. Dr. Clifford Hawkins and Dr. Ron Howard provided valuable suggestions on the sections dealing with medical meetings and medical terminology. Nigel Bruce, Hideo Masuda, and Patrick Barron have been a generous source of ideas. My special thanks go to former colleagues at the English Language Institute, University of Michigan, especially Larry Selinker, Cathy Pettinari, Dan Douglas, and Joan Morley; the Institute for Applied Language Studies, University of Edinburgh, especially Joan Maclean and Lesley Shield; Edinburgh Language Foundation, especially Beverly Holmstrom and Eric Glendinning; Shimane Medical University, especially Chuzo Mori; De La Salle University, Manila, especially Glenda Fortez and Andrea Penaflorida. My thanks also to Dr. Henry Walton at the World Federation for Medical Education. Needless to say, all errors are mine.

I am most grateful to my wife, Aya, to whom this book is dedicated, and whose medical professionalism and good judgment have been a constant support.

J.C.M.

Speaking at Medical Meetings:
Anatomy of the Presentation

A talk can be divided into several sections or, to use a musical analogy, different "movements." There is a beginning, a middle, and an end. The thread of purpose should be carried clearly throughout the presentation, with indications along the way of the main focus of the paper and a closing "finale" in which the speaker returns to the main theme once again. Also, when the speaker needs to move from one section to another, or even from one point to another, there must be some signal to the listeners that this shift is taking place.

Study the divisions of a presentation and try to identify how the speaker marks them (or fails to do so) by the language used. In the following pages the language used in various sections of a talk is described in detail.

Greetings

It is usual to greet an audience simply. Some speakers may make a humorous comment, but if you are not confident about this then it is best to avoid it. Thank the chairperson, greet your listeners, then begin. Look at these three sequenced steps.

1. Good morning.
2. Thank you, Mr. Chairman, and good afternoon, ladies and gentlemen.
3. I'd like, first of all, to thank the organizers of this meeting for inviting me here this evening. It is also a particular pleasure for me to pay my first visit to this beautiful city.

Opening Remarks

This is the point of departure when the speaker introduces the topic of the presentation. It is acceptable to expand briefly on the title: but without going into detail. Any slight changes that have been made to the title or theme of the paper should be introduced here. Consider these options:

1. The title of my presentation is . . . .
2. I'd like to talk today about . . . .
3. My topic today is . . . .
4. My subject today is . . . .

The Plan

It is important at the beginning to outline to the audience the scope of the talk and to describe the order in which the main points will be made.

1. I have divided my talk into four sections . . . .
   I have divided the subject into four sections . . . .
2. The first point I am going to make concerns . . . .
   My first point concerns . . . .
   The first point I'd like to make is . . . .
   The first part of my talk will concern . . . .
   I'd like firstly to talk about . . . .
3. My second point concerns . . . .
   The second part will concern . . . .
4. My third point concerns . . . .
   In the third part I deal with the question of . . . .
5. Finally, I'd like to talk a little about . . . .
   And finally, I shall raise briefly the issue of . . . .
   Finally, I shall address the problem of . . . .

Opening the Main Section

1. Let me start by posing the question . . . .
2. I'd like to begin by suggesting that . . . .
3. I'd like to start by drawing your attention to . . . .
4. Let me begin by noting that . . . .

Moving to a New Point

"Signaling" that a new point is being introduced provides the listeners with a "breathing space." They are given the opportunity to reflect for a moment on the previous point and prepare for a new one. Pausing for a few seconds is a useful way of dividing one section or point from another. This can be accompanied by one of several verbal expressions.

1. Let me now turn to . . . .
2. I'd like to turn now to the question of . . . .
3. Let me turn now to the issue of . . . .
4. Moving on now to the question of . . . .
5. If we now look at . . . .
6. Let's look now at the question of . . . .
7. Having looked at this subject let's now turn to . . . .
8. Can we now turn to . . . .

Elaborating a Point

"Elaborating" expressions show that you are going to develop a point in more detail or expand it into a main issue.

1. I'd like to look at this in a bit more detail.
2. Can I develop this point a bit further?

3. Let me elaborate on this point.
4. Let's look at this problem in a bit more detail.
5. The first aspect of this problem is . . . .

Postponing

Sometimes during a talk you may need to delay description of a point until later on. Certain expressions indicate that you will not deal with a particular topic immediately, but will return to it later in the talk.

1. I'll be returning to this point later.
2. I'll be coming back to this point later.
3. As I'll show later . . . .
4. I'll come to this later.
5. As will be shown later . . . .
6. Later, I'll come to . . . .
7. Later, I'll be coming back to . . . .

Referring Back

A speaker, during the course of a talk, may refer to some previous point or theme. This is a useful device, for it gives a sense of continuity and wholeness to the talk. By referring back, a speaker may recycle important information and provide greater coherence to the development of the talk.

1. Getting back to the question of . . . .
2. Coming back now to the issue which I raised earlier . . . .
3. Can I now go back to the question I posed at the beginning?
4. As I said earlier . . . .
5. As I mentioned earlier . . . .
6. As we saw earlier . . . .
7. I'd like now to return to the question . . . .
8. As you will remember . . . .

Highlighting

There is a group of expressions that may help the speaker bring certain points to the foreground. They have the effect of verbally underlining an issue or creating unusual contrast for a particular point.

1. The interesting thing about . . . is . . . .
2. The significant thing about . . . is . . . .
3. The important thing about . . . is . . . .
4. The thing to remember is . . . .
5. What you have to remember is . . . .
6. What we have to realize is . . . .
7. What I find most interesting about . . . is . . . .
8. Strangely enough . . . .
9. Funnily enough . . . .
10. Oddly enough . . . .

Indicators

This group of expressions serves to indicate that a point or section has been
satisfactorily completed and that a new point will be made. Alternatively,
it may simply provide the speaker with a kind of springboard on which to
pause before continuing.

1. Okay . . . .
2. Right . . . .
3. Right then . . . .
4. Good . . . .
5. Now . . . .
6. Now then . . . .
7. Well . . . .
8. Well now . . . .
9. Well then . . . .

Summarizing

Toward the end of a talk it becomes necessary to sum up. The main aim of
the talk should be recalled and the major points touched upon. Obviously,
it is unwise to introduce new information in this final section.

1. The main points that have been made are . . . .
2. Let me try now to pull the main threads of this argument together.
3. In conclusion I should just like to say . . . .
4. Just before concluding I'd like to say . . . .
5. Summing up then . . . .
6. By way of summary, the main points in the study seem to me to
   be . . . .
7. To sum up then . . . .

Thanking the Audience

1. Thank you.
2. I'll finish there. Thank you.
3. And let me finish there. Thank you.

Speaking at Medical Meetings:
A Checklist

Speaking in public is a skill. The presentation of a scientific paper requires special preparation, both linguistic and material. You may know the subject of your talk thoroughly, but your presentation may be incomprehensible for a number of reasons. When speaking it is important to try to be clear, interesting, concise, and confident. Speaking in public in a foreign language can be doubly stressful and poses particular problems. The lecturer may, for instance, try to overcome nervousness about pronunciation by speaking too quickly, or even too deliberately. The talk may be read verbatim instead of presented in a more loose-textured way. The dangers here are lack of eye contact with the audience, a rigid stance on the platform, and a monotone delivery. If the paper is read, therefore, instead of using notes, special preparation is necessary to make it varied and interesting, and to give a sense of real interaction with the listeners.

When preparing your talk, refer to this checklist and consider the points it raises about your presentation:

1. Have you *rehearsed* your talk?
   ❏ Yes   ❏ No
2. Have you kept in mind the *type of audience* you are addressing (i.e., specialist, nonspecialist, lay)?
   ❏ Yes   ❏ No
3. Have you *made arrangements* for the provision of visual aids (e.g., overhead projector, slide projector) if necessary?
   ❏ Yes   ❏ No
4. Have you looked at (when possible) the *lecture room* and podium?
   ❏ Yes   ❏ No
5. Does the *title* of your paper reflect its true purpose?
   ❏ Yes   ❏ No
6. How will you *greet* the audience?
   ?   ❏ Don't know
7. Are the *goals* of your paper made clear in the introduction?
   ❏ Yes   ❏ No
8. How will the audience be able to *follow the main points*?
   ?   ❏ Don't know

13

9. Is your talk *organized* into *sections* or *points*?
   ❏ Yes   ❏ No
10. How do you *signal* when changing topic or moving on to a new point?
    ?   ❏ Don't know
11. Have you considered using *visual aids* to make the talk more clear, varied, and interesting (slides, overhead projector, tape recorder, video)?
    ❏ Yes   ❏ No
12. Are the slides or overhead projector acetates *difficult to read* from the back row of the lecture room?
    ❏ Yes   ❏ No
13. Are there *handouts* to make your talk easier to follow (especially when dealing with complex data)?
    ❏ Yes   ❏ No
14. Is the *loudness* appropriate (with or without microphone)?
    ❏ Yes   ❏ No
15. Do you *interact* appropriately with the audience (e.g., eye contact, facial expression)?
    ❏ Yes   ❏ No
16. Do you use appropriate *body language* (relaxed stance, gestures)?
    ❏ Yes   ❏ No
17. Is the *amount of information* appropriate (too much, too little)?
    ❏ Yes   ❏ No
18. Is the *speed* of your talk appropriate?
    ❏ Yes   ❏ No
19. Do you need to check the *pronunciation* of certain expressions?
    ❏ Yes   ❏ No
20. Have you checked the *grammar* of your paper?
    ❏ Yes   ❏ No
21. List below the basic weaknesses of your presentation. (Try to do this exercise both before and after your talk.) Use the points raised in this checklist to help you specify the features that need revising.

_____   _____

_____   _____

_____   _____

_____   _____

Conference and Seminar Discussion

This section deals with the language of formal meetings. During meetings participants express ideas and opinions, argue, disagree, interrupt, and change their minds. The expressions given here are suitable for the formal, polite speech of seminars and conferences. Of course, many of the expressions can also be heard in daily, casual conversation.

Entering the Discussion

Could I (just) say something about . . . ?
Could I (just) come in at this point?
I'd like to pick up one of the last speaker's points.

Agreeing

I agree.
I quite agree.
I think you're absolutely right.
I couldn't agree more.
I think the speaker is right in what he says.
You've got a very good point there.

I'd go along with you { there. / on that.

I take your point (that . . .).

Yes, I'd tend to agree with you { there. / on that.

On the whole, I think the speaker's arguments are fair.

Disagreeing, Doubting, Attacking

I'm afraid I can't agree with Dr. X on this { matter. / point.

I'm not sure that I entirely agree with Dr. X.
I'm afraid I'm not convinced.
By and large, I would accept the speaker's views, but . . . .

I'm not sure if I would { agree / go along } with you { that . . . . / there. / on that.

I can see your point, but . . . .
I'm not so sure about that.
I don't think I'd say that.
Yes, but don't you think . . . ?
I'd like to reserve judgment on that.
I'd agree with you to a certain extent, but . . . .
I was a bit worried about . . . .
I got the feeling that . . . .
Dr. X's paper was very interesting, but I wonder if she has
    considered . . . .
Isn't it (also) true to say that . . . ?
Don't you think that . . . .
Might it not (also) be true that . . . ?
Isn't it just possible that . . . ?
Wouldn't you agree that . . . ?
Would you agree that . . . ?

Answering Doubts and Attacks

That's an interesting point, but . . . .
Yes, I get your point. But even so . . . .
I see what you mean. But, with respect, we refuted that in . . . .
Yes, I see that. But I don't see where that point comes into it.
Yes, I see that. But is it relevant?

Stalling and Hedging

I'm not (quite) sure what you mean.
Could we come back to that?
Could you (Would you care to) elaborate on that point?
It remains to be seen whether . . . .
Well, (I must admit) it's rather difficult to say.
What do other people think about this?
Perhaps we can ask for other people's views on this?

Asking for Clarification or More Information

I'm sorry, could you say that again?
I'm afraid I didn't quite get the speaker's last point. Could she go
    over it again?
Am I correct in assuming . . . ?
I'm sorry, I don't quite understand what you mean by . . . ?
I'm sorry, could you explain what you mean by . . . ?
I'm afraid I'm not very clear about what you mean by . . . .

Giving Clarification or More Information

[Well,] what I'm trying to say is that . . . .

[Well,] the point I'm trying to make is that . . . .
[Well,] I suppose what I'm saying is that . . . .
What I mean is that . . . .
What I'm suggesting is that . . . .
To put it another way . . . .

Changing Your Mind

On reflection, I think that Dr. X was perhaps right when she
    said . . . .
I'd like to withdraw what I said about . . . .
I think I was probably mistaken when I said that . . . .

Asking for Opinions

How do you feel about . . . ?
What do you think of . . . ?
What is your opinion of . . . ?
I was wondering how you felt about . . . ?
I was wondering where you stand on the question of . . . ?
What about . . . ?

Expressing Opinions

In my opinion . . . .
It seems to me that . . . .
In my view . . . .
From my point of view . . . .
As far as I can see . . . .
As far as I'm able to judge . . . .

Making Suggestions

Do you not think it might be $\left\{\begin{array}{l}\text{better}\\\text{more sensible}\\\text{more advisable}\end{array}\right\}$ to . . . .

Do you not think it would be a good idea to . . . ?
Mightn't it be rather better to . . . ?
What about . . . ?

Anticipating Criticism

Let me lay to rest any possible fears by saying that . . . .
Well, of course, it could be objected that . . . . But . . . .
    However . . . .
Now, I'm sure you would want to point out that . . . .
I think we have anticipated some of the possible/potential problems.

Conference "Coffee Break" Conversation

For many people attending a scientific conference, intermissions such as coffee break in the morning, lunch, and the conference dinner are important opportunities for meeting colleagues, renewing acquaintances, and generally exchanging ideas in an informal atmosphere. Nevertheless, carrying on an informal conversation between colleagues can prove, for some nonnative speakers of English, as equally formidable a challenge as presenting a paper! Let us say, for example, that you want to start up a conversation with someone whom you think you've met before at a previous conference (but are not certain). How do you do it? Here are a few conversational "ice breakers" for a variety of situations to help you get started.

Meeting an Old Friend (Casual Style)

Karen: Stella! Good to see you again.
Stella: Hi, Karen! How are you?
Karen: Oh, pretty good. You weren't at Athens. How are things?
Stella: Mm. Pretty good. Oh . . . er . . . thanks for the Christmas card . . . .

Meeting an Old Friend (Casual Style)

Masa: Olaf! Hello there.
Olaf: Masa! Long time no see.
Masa: I looked for you at Registration.
Olaf: Well, I got here late. Missed the plenary session in fact.

Meeting an Old Friend/Aquaintance (Formal Style)

Dr. Schippers: Ah! Dr. Greaves. Nice to see you again.
Dr. Greaves: Dr. Schippers. How nice to see you. I was hoping we might see each other again.
Dr. Schippers: Yes, it must be . . . let's see . . . a year ago since the Edinburgh conference.
Dr. Greaves: That's right. September, wasn't it? Anyway, how . . . er . . . how is the Monica project going?

Meeting an Old Friend/Aquaintance (Semi-formal Style)

Utako: Hello, Karl! Good to see you again.

Karl: Hi, Utako! How are you?

Utako: I'm very well indeed. And how about you?

Karl: Very well, thank you. Actually, I'm a bit surprised to see you here. I thought you'd be at the Vienna seminar. You had a paper accepted, didn't you?

Utako: Well, actually, I heard that Selvini was speaking at this conference, so I decided to come here instead.

Approaching a Conference Speaker (Not Met Previously)

Dr. Barron: Dr. Maurice, I enjoyed your paper very much.

Dr. Maurice: Well, that's kind of you to say so. Thank you. I don't believe we've met.

Dr. Barron: No, I'm Paul Barron from Glasgow.

Dr. Maurice: Oh, are you working with Jan Fisiak on the Alzheimer's project?

Dr. Barron: That's right.

Dr. Maurice: Well, tell me, how is it getting along?

Dr. Barron: Very well indeed. At the moment . . . .

Approaching a Conference Speaker – Introducing Your Work

Dr. Lichtenstein: Dr. Giertz, that was a very interesting paper this morning. Thank you.

Dr. Giertz: Well, thank you for saying so.

Dr. Lichtenstein: As a matter of fact, I'm working on an area very close to yours I think – eosinophil chemotactic activity.

Dr. Giertz: I'm sorry, I didn't catch your name.

Dr. Lichtenstein: Oh, I'm sorry; Jim Lichtenstein from Stuttgart . . . University of Stuttgart.

Dr. Giertz: Walter Giertz. Please call me Walter. Let's try and find a seat and chat . . . .

Approaching a Conference Speaker – Asking Supplementary Questions

Dr. Okamoto: Dr. Austen, thank you for a very interesting paper. I was wondering if I could ask you a question?

Dr. Austen: Go right ahead.

Approaching a Conference Speaker – Asking a Supplementary Question and Introducing Yourself

Dr. Jagdish: Dr. Calvini, I enjoyed your paper very much.

Dr. Calvini: Well, thank you.

Dr. Jagdish: Lucy Jagdish from Moorfields, London.

Dr. Calvini: Pleased to meet you.

Dr. Jagdish: Actually, I was wondering if I might ask you a couple of questions about the work you're doing on . . . .

Reintroducing Yourself (to Someone Who Has Forgotten Your Name)

Dr. Hanson: Dr. Napaporn, hello! I wonder if you remember me?

Dr. Napaporn: Oh . . . er . . . .

Dr. Hanson: Jon Hanson from Sydney . . . we met in Bangkok last year.

Dr. Napaporn: Yes, of course. I'm sorry. My mind went blank for a moment. How are you, Dr. Hanson?

Inviting Someone to Visit Your University/Hospital (Exchanging Name Cards)

Dr. Kim: Dr. Sweeney, we haven't met, but I'm Joon Kim from Yonsei, Seoul. My name card.

Dr. Sweeney: How do you do, Dr. Kim. I'm terribly sorry but I've somehow run out of cards.

Dr. Kim: That's okay. Don't bother. Er . . . actually I'm very glad to be able to speak to you personally. We're opening a new Institute of Mental Health in Seoul. I know that you've just opened a similar institute in Dublin. I read your reports on it in the *British Medical Journal*.

Dr. Sweeney: Oh yes. It was quite a headache getting started.

Dr. Kim: Well, actually, I'd very much like to talk to you about that. I'm head of the planning committee for the new center, and I wonder if it might be possible for you to come to Seoul and talk to our team?

Dr. Sweeney: Well, that sounds very interesting. Maybe we should sit down somewhere and talk it over?

Dr. Kim: Good. There's a quiet spot over there.

A Selection of Conversational "Ice Breakers"/ Casual Exchanges

1. Standing in the "Coffee Line"

A. Well, I thought it was a good presentation.

B. I thought so too.
A. Danielle Baetens from Brussels.
B. Elvira Castades, Madrid.

2. Standing in the "Coffee Line"

A. I saw you taking masses of notes. You were sitting in front of me.
B. Aha. Yes, I was interested in the topic.
A. I'm Alice Mervi from Helsinki.
B. How do you do. Jenny Macfarland from Dundee, Scotland.

3. Looking for a Room

A. Excuse me, do you know where Pier Haugen's presentation is?
B. I'm sorry, no. Try at the Reception Desk over there.
A. Thank you. Sorry to bother you.
B. No problem.
A. Excuse me, could you tell me in which room is the Haugen presentation?

4. Asking about the "Conference Banquet"

A. Excuse me, I haven't registered for the conference banquet yet.
B. Yes, we do have some tickets left.
A. Good, I'll take two.
B. Okay. Could I have your name?
A. Kabira. That's K-A-B-I-R-A. Initial J.
B. Fine, Dr. Kabira. That's 7 p.m. in the Willow Room. And that will be $40.

The Anatomy of a Medical Paper

TITLE

A title is not a sentence in the familiar sense of having a subject, verb, and object with one or two dependent clauses. Frequently, for example, there is no verb in the title.

The title should be concise but informative, containing the key words of the paper. It is supposed to describe in as few words as possible the content of the paper. A title must be specific. "An Investigation of Mast Cell Functioning" is not as specific as "The Role of Mast Cells in Inflammation," even though it is about the same length.

Often, the first words of a title state the general field of inquiry ("Obesity:"/"Measles Immunization:"/"Recurrent Cerebellitis–") followed by a colon (:) or dash (–). Then specific details are given to the right of the colon. For example: "Adult Respiratory Distress Syndrome: How Many Cases in Canada?"

Often, the main point of the investigation is stated immediately in the title. The pattern of the study emerges in expressions such as:

Treatment of . . .	Diagnosis of . . .
Measurement of . . .	Study of . . .
Effect of/on . . .	Management of . . .
Role of . . .	Implications of/for . . .
Trial of . . .	Contribution of . . .
Investigation of . . .	Survey of . . .
Evaluation of . . .	Analysis of . . .
Assessment of . . .	Influence of . . .
Impact of . . .	

In some titles a problem may be presented, then followed by a description of the cause. An example of this is given below. Note the use of expressions like "due to" and "resulting from": "Carotid Stenosis Due to Clamp Injury."

Note the frequent reference to where a disease or analysis occurs. In other words, if you are dealing with carcinoma then you will probably say whether it is 'in the liver' or 'in the lung' and so on. Similarly, you may need to state the parameters of your study in the title by referring to the nature or location of the population. Consider these examples:

"Testicular Carcinoma *In Situ* in Children with Androgen Insensitivity Syndrome"

"The Effect of Wartime Starvation in Holland upon Pregnancy and Its Product"

"Vidarabine Versus Acyclovir Therapy in Herpes Simplex"

"Infective Endocarditis: With an Analysis of 150 Cases with Special Reference to the Chronic Form of the Disease"

"Income Problems in the Homecare of Intellectually Handicapped Children"

"Endoscopic Correction of Primary Vesico-ureteric Reflux: Results in 94 Ureters"

ABSTRACT

* The length of an abstract may be anything from 50 to 200 words. To some extent, length depends on how extensive the topic of the paper is, and how complicated or numerous the results are. However, check the "guidelines" or "instructions" to authors for possible details about maximum length of abstract.

* An abstract states the *purpose* or *specific objectives* of the study or investigation. For instance, it might be a study of the parents of mentally handicapped children "to determine factors that might influence psychiatric morbidity." The objective might be to compare X with Y in the following:

"The efficiency of the spatula in obtaining dyskaryotic cells and improving the cellular quality of smears was compared with that of the Ayre spatula in a controlled trial."

* An abstract usually indicates the basic *methodology* used, e.g., the number and type of patients involved, experimental animals, observational and analytic methods:

"A total of 1849 boys born to mothers who are residents of a defined area around Oxford were examined for cryptorchidism."

"A total of 748 patients who attended four south London group practices were screened using the eating attitude test."

"In a cross-sectional study the mental health of parents of physically and mentally handicapped preschool children was compared with that of parents of healthy preschool children."

* The *main results* will be found in the abstract. This may include a brief summary of the data and statistical significance where necessary. For example:

"Seventy percent (549) of the patients had been treated within one week, treatment having started on the same day for 8.5 perzcent (67) of the patients. This compares with a mean of six weeks for . . . ."

* Principal *conclusions* are stated clearly and briefly without lengthy discussion. A conclusion might be *definitive*, as in these examples:

"Tranexamic acid reduces the blood transfusion requirement and need for emergency surgery in patients bleeding from a benign gastric or duodenal lesion."

"It seems certain, therefore, that in cases such as these, cerebral angiography is advisable to exclude vascular damage."

"The causes of false negative results in tuberculin tests have been listed as faulty tuberculin material, faulty administration, and inadequate interpretation of the response or rapid dissipation of tuberculin due to local inflammation. To this list we now add blunted skin puncture needles. Failure to inspect the puncture gun routinely may lead to potentially serious consequences."

A conclusion may be *hedged* in which the author carefully avoids giving a direct and strong commitment to a position or point of view but without seeming to be too vague. Look at these examples:

"Of course, both possibilities remain: fracture due to the machine itself or to an inherent weakness in the shaft of the distal humerus. It may not be possible to determine which of these factors is most influential in this case although our investigation seems to point toward some structural defect in the design of lever of the machine."

"We cannot help but wonder whether this theory has outlived its usefulness. Hypothalamic abnormality may, indeed, play a crucial part. Our own experience suggests that less elaborate explanations, invoking social and personal factors, seem more sensible."

INTRODUCTION

The introduction presents the purpose and scope of the report. This is the place for a brief review of related literature. Unless you are writing an M.D. thesis, a long review with references is not appropriate. The method of investigation and a statement of the principal conclusions are presented in this section. We can, therefore, divide the "introduction" into several components.

An introduction may first display a *definition of terms*. An unfamiliar term, or an expression that is being assigned a different meaning from the usual one, must be explained; or an author might simply wish to remind the reader what the term is generally understood to mean. Consider this example: "Dialysis arthropathy is a complication of long term hemodialysis. It is predominantly bilateral, affecting both large and small joints, and is strongly associated with recurrent carpal tunnel syndrome." And again, "Hypomagnesemia is a well-known association of diabetes mellitus; it is often asymptomatic and . . . ."

Background to the subject matter includes a general statement that orients the reader to the area of research with which the paper deals. For example: "There is increasing evidence that atrialnatriuretic peptides are an important hormonal system for the regulation of sodium and water balance."

Review of Previous Research

What research has been done in this field? What advances have been made? What are the outstanding problems? These are the types of questions that may be dealt with in an introduction. Review of the literature often takes the following forms:

> "Many reports have appeared in journals or general practice and have been well reviewed."

> "Soluit and Clark characterized the response of parents to the birth of their defective child as mourning the death of their fanta-sized perfect child."

Notice the frequent use of the present perfect tense and the simple past tense when reviewing research. For example, "Vesico-ureteric reflux has been reported in one third to a half of children. . . ."

> "The results of recent work have suggested that patients with ulcerative colitis. . . ."

> "Parker (1989) in Australia reported this age difference."

Whereas the present perfect form is used with nonspecific time relating to previous events (e.g., research), the past simple indicates reference to specific research completed by X in a particular year. For example:

> "Several studies have appeared in this journal (Walton, 1987)."

> "Borderline syndrome has been the focus of many studies which . . . ."

> "Nayha (1988) in Finland noted that the disease was more widespread . . . ."

Reporting Expressions

Note the use of verbs of reporting in this section.

> . . . has been reported.
> . . . was reported.
> . . . was described.

The Knowledge Gap

It is common in the introduction to indicate the existence of a gap in research or knowledge about the subject being discussed. It is precisely for this reason that the author is presenting his or her own observations. A knowledge or information gap is commonly expressed thus:

> "In the United Kingdom there have been few studies of . . . ."

> "This problem seems to have been overlooked in the research because . . . ."

Statement of Purpose

Following a description of the knowledge gap there is typically a statement of intent or purpose which explains how such a gap is to be "filled," re-analyzed, or even widened in scope.

"The most widely accepted hypothesis that public health is solely dependent upon state finance must, therefore, be reexamined . . . ."

METHODS

Materials and Methods : Patients and Methods : Subjects and Methods

The word *materials* refers to the use of laboratory apparatus or experimental animals. If a report deals with patients, then the section will be headed "Patients and Methods" rather than "Materials and Methods." The author should identify correctly the methods, the apparatus (the name and address of the manufacturer given in brackets), drugs and chemicals, patients, experimental animals, plants, and microorganisms used in the study. Mentioned in this section are the statistical significance of findings and numbers of observations.

The Sample

At the outset, the author describes the nature and size of the sample (patients, specimens, etc.) that has been studied. The precise type and number are identified.

"Two hundred and forty brains obtained by necropsy were studied in collaboration with the forensic pathologists of the Perth city coroner's department."

Time/Period of the Investigation

Over what period of time was the study completed? This information may be of importance for an understanding of the study and is obviously essential in longitudinal studies.

"Between April 1981 and December 1985, 120 patients with stones in the common bile duct were entered into a prospective study in which patients . . . ."

"From August 1, 1981 to July 31, 1983, all deaths in which the coroner's report, or part one of the death certificate, contained the word *asthma* or *asthmatic* were investigated."

"Each participating physician had to recruit at least 10 people aged 65 years or more over a two month period."

Location

Details may be given about the place where the study was undertaken.

"Twelve consecutive patients with intrahepatic cholestasis of pregnancy from the antenatal ward, and 12 healthy pregnant women

from the out-patient maternity center, were studied."
"Between January 1978 and June 1985, 95 patients with severe
hidradenitis were treated by wide excisional surgery in this de-
partment."
"The patient, aged 36, was referred to King's College Hospital,
London, at 11 weeks' gestation."

Procedures

There are numerous methods of data collection. The selection of the most
suitable one is obviously dependent upon many factors: size of the sample,
nature of the investigation, and so on. In large-scale studies, a questionnaire is frequently used as a measurement technique. In a clinical trial, the
method of analysis may be blood-sampling, biopsy, or X-ray. Notice the
almost exclusive use of the passive construction when describing analytical procedures. Expressions such as:

blood *was collected* with a plastic syringe
serum *was transferred*
exudates *were drawn* with a disposable plastic pipette
exudate *was eluted*
samples *were transported*
samples *were screened* by radioimmunoassay
antigens *were extracted* from clinical specimens in TN
the detergent *was removed* by two extractions with S volumes of
     ether
rubella virus *was grown and purified* as previously described
the filter *was incubated* for 16 hours in the same buffer
hemoagglutination inhibition testing *was performed*
the samples *were checked* microscopically and frozen
tissue specimens *were teased out* in 2ml of Medium 199
tissue specimens *were innoculated* into four replicate cultures
the cells *were incubated*
the supernatant from positive cultures *was dialyzed* against coating
serum *was fractionated* by ion exchange chromatography
all patients *were interviewed and examined* in their own homes
the patient *was also seen* by a neurologist
diagnosis *was based* on the finding of one or two
patients *were asked* to rate their symptoms using visual analogue
     scales
three standardized self-rating questionnaires *were used*
patients *were allocated* to a diagnostic category on the basis of
data *were analyzed* in two ways
dementia *was assessed* using the Aberdeen minimental state
     questionnaire

Data Analysis

Authors outline how data was analyzed in the study without necessarily going on to describe the results of the analysis. In other words, what tests or measurements were used and what were the most important variables are featured in the Methods section. For example:

"Incidence ratios were calculated separately for each category, and, where appropriate, linear tests for trend were carried out using a standard method."

"For each recorded activity they were required to rate on a scale of 1–10 their general mood, anxiety/tension, and anger/frustration. On the scale for general mood, 1 represented extreme unhappiness and 10 complete joy."

"Differences between the two groups were analyzed by X^2 or the student's t test. As factors could be correlated with each other, a multivariate analysis was also performed using stepwise logistic regression (Biomedical data package statistical software)."

RESULTS

In this section authors present the most important observations, putting the results in logical or chronological order. The results are displayed, where appropriate, in tables and diagrams.

Analyzing the Sample

The first step in describing the results of a study or observation is to state in more detail, for example, by statistical analysis, the various features of the sample population, and to restate the period covered by the research. As in the Materials and Methods section, there is much use of the passive construction and the simple past tense.

For example:

"A total of 1879 eligible boys were born alive in the 12 months of the study; 1837 (97.9%) were born in the John Radcliffe Hospital, and we examined 1803 (98.1%) of them soon after birth."

"Of the 317 patients who attended the unit during the study, 106 were unable to complete the questionnaires: 70 were demented or unable to comprehend the questions; 12 had multiple sclerosis; 8 did not have a sufficient grasp of English; 11 did not have their reading glasses; and 5 refused."

"Of the 120 patients, five were incorrectly entered into the trial; two had a complicated diagnosis (cholangiocarcinoma and acute appendicitis with liver abcess, respectively), one was under the care of a consultant not participating in the trial, one refused operation, and another refused endoscopic retrograde cholangiopancreatography."

Data Analysis

Following a brief analysis of the research, sample data gathered from the sample is further analyzed, most commonly from a statistical point of view. The results can then be seen clearly and definitively.

Notice that in the case of questionnaire-based research one paragraph has dealt with the numbers of respondents who did not complete a questionnaire or who did not participate in the research (see above: Analyzing the Sample). One can then expect the author to go on to deal with the actual results from the data available.

"Questionnaires were completed by 211 patients (mean age 46.6 years, range 15–79). The most frequent diagnosis was genuine stress incontinence (66 patients [31%]). Fifty-two patients (25%) had sensory urgency or detrusor instability . . . ."

"There were no substantial differences in initial characteristics among the three study groups (Table 1). More people, however, added salt at the table in group 1 than in the two other groups ($X1^2$ = 5.2; $p < 0.05$)."

"3-Methylhistidine excretion fell when subjects ate a vegetarian diet, and rose again in group 2 on return to an omnivorous diet. Similarly, urinary urea was lower after subjects had been taking the vegetarian diet for six weeks."

DISCUSSION

What is new, original, and important about the investigation? Does it agree or disagree with other published work? What are the implications of the findings and what are their limitations (lack of correlation, for instance)? These questions are addressed in this final section. It is important to connect the conclusions to the goals of the study and, if necessary, suggest new hypotheses – perhaps toward a further examination of some aspect of the study.

Confirmation

The results may or may not be what was expected by the author. Therefore some comment will be made about whether the results are valid, significant (in a statistical or nonstatistical sense) and helpful in solving a problem or confirming a hypothesis. For example:

"Our data, therefore, confirm that general practice is the main interface between . . . ."

"Our analysis of the epidemiological studies taken together shows an increased risk of lung cancer in . . . ."

"Suggestions that human plasma contains substances capable of causing immunosuppression have been made by others, and we believe our data support this hypothesis."

Restatement of Reason for Research

Why was the study undertaken? What were the problems or previous deficiencies in knowledge about the subject that provoked the need for research? The Discussion section addresses these questions and especially may remind the reader of its initial criticisms. For example:

"The term *bronchial hyper-activity* has been widely used in the past without having been defined operationally."

The Importance of the Study

The discussion section emphasizes the importance of the research and its contribution to that area of study. It shows its value in supplementing or replacing previous work. For example:

"To our knowledge, ours is the first prospective study of Rh negative women who had . . . ."

"Another point highlighted by this survey was that only a few patients . . . ."

Implications for Future Research

The discussion may include suggestions for further research concerning the theme of the article, or on the need for more research on some specific aspect of the study. Consider these examples:

"Further studies are needed, however, to clarify the nature of bronchial irritability syndrome."

"Future studies should concentrate on how, and whence, pathogenic micro-organisms acquire iron *in vivo*."

"It will be interesting to see how widespread this mechanism is among bacteria, and to learn more about it."

"Clearly, more controlled studies on low-dose maintenance medication for schizophrenia will be required. Nevertheless, the concept should gain popularity—among both patients and physicians."

Hedging

An author may not want to state something too definitely or concretely. The writer might simply wish to suggest an interpretation or point to a likelihood. This is a strategy for writing about data which not only allows for the possibility of alternative interpretations, but also partly shelters the author from strong criticism. Conversely, authors may actually hedge criticism of the research of others by expressions of 'doubt' rather than of outright dismissal. Typical hedging expressions employed by writers are:

It is possible that . . . .
It is likely that . . . .

It is probable that . . . .
Our data suggest that . . . .
Most probably, any patient exposed to . . . .
Our experience suggests that . . . .
These findings suggest that . . . .
These data point to the possibility that . . . . It may be the case
that . . . .
We must now consider the possibility that . . . .
A probable explanation for this is that . . . .
Here are some further examples in context:

"Our data suggest that previous studies might usefully be re-examined to see what kinds of blood components were given."

"We think it likely that some substances in homologous plasma cause reduced immune function in patients with cancer given whole blood."

"It is doubtful whether these mucin changes are tumor specific, as they have been reported in inflammatory bowel conditions in man."

Figures, Diagrams, Tables

There are several ways of referring, within the text, to accompanying figures and tables in the Results section. The purpose of such figures is to provide a clear and readily understandable visual display of information that would otherwise require lengthy and complex explanation. Reference will therefore be of a precise nature pointing out the function of the information displayed, and not just the fact that it is there. For example:

"Table 2 contrasts the childhood leukemia registration ratios in . . . with . . . ."

"Figures 2 and 3 show the distribution of childhood leukemia in . . . ."

"Tables 4 and 5 summarize the evidence for the increased incidence of . . . .'

"The results (Fig. 1a) show that the patient's serum did contain a low level of . . . ."

"The patient's serum hemagglutination inhibition titer at the time of termination had dropped to 1/128 (see Table), and virus specific IgM was . . . ."

"Table 1 gives the doctors' characteristics by age group."

"Table 4 provides the number of reports of adverse drug reactions . . . ."

Catalogue of Sample Sentences:
The "TAIMRAD" Structure

Here is a bank of model sentences from each section of a medical journal article. You may wish to consult these sentences when you come to write or practice writing your own reports. It is useful, also, to analyze the structure of these examples, referring to the scheme or "anatomy" outlined above. It should be possible to identify some of the typical features of the TAIMRAD structure* in the sample sentences. You may also begin to notice other characteristics of this scheme.

TITLES

– The role of calcium in human cutaneous anaphylaxis

– Effect of heparin on histaminase in guinea pig skin

– Treatment of pleuroperitoneal hernia in the newborn–with special reference to cardiorespiratory disturbances

– Transition of biparietal diameters at antenatal and postnatal periods

– Gas chromatography study on effect of nitrazepam on Aminobutyric acid in mouse brain

– Two cases of Haroda's syndrome, including one preceded by symptoms of glaucoma

– Brain biopsy for suspected herpes simplex encephalitis: a case report on vagotomy and acid secretion

– Recurrent cerebellitis – A case report of a possible relationship with Epstein-Barr infection

– Evaluation of the enzyme-linked immunosorbent assay (Toxo ELISA test kit) for the diagnosis of toxoplasmosis

– Obesity: New insight into the anthropometric classification of fat distribution shown by computed tomography

– Measles immunization: Results of a local program to increase vaccine uptake

*TAIMRAD = Title, Abstracts, Introduction, Methods, Results, and Discussion

- Computer assisted screening: Effect on the patient and his consultation
- Is repeated flushing of Hickman catheters necessary?
- Chest physiotherapy in primary pneumonia
- Cluster headfacha and herpes simplex: An association?
- Risk factors for death in complicated diarrhea of children
- Delay in diagnosing testicular tumors
- A case-control study of cervical cancer screening in northeast Scotland
- Adverse cardiovascular response to oral trimeprazine in children
- Accidental digitalis poisoning due to drinking herbal tea

ABSTRACTS

- An attempt was made to replicate in the USA sex differences reported for the seasonal distribution of suicide in the UK, Finland, and Australia. No sex differences were found. Spring and late summer peaks were found for suicides by both males and females. The method of suicide was found to be an important factor in the seasonal distribution of the suicides of males and females.
- We examined like and unlike sex twinning rates in Great Britain by social class over the period 1974–85. Although twinning rates are believed to have changed over that period, we found no evidence of differential change by social class, suggesting that any factors affecting twinning are widespread in the population.
- This is a detailed autopsy case of rare juvenile parkinsonism with dominant heredity. The patient displayed parkinsonian symptoms which began at the age of 24, and expired in a state of quadriplegia-in-flexion at 35. In the later stage, myclonijerks . . . The autopsy revealed severe degeneration and . . . This case was considered to belong essentially to idiopathic parkinsonism. The pathology of juvenile parkinsonism is reviewed briefly.
- The assessments by radiographers of 1628 consecutive patients referred for radiography in the casualty department were analyzed.
- The relation between cholesterol concentration and mortality was studied prospectively over 17 years in 630 New Zealand Maoris aged 25–74.
- A search of the Home Office index of notified drug addicts identified 1499 deaths during 1967–81, of which 226 (15%) were of therapeutic addicts – that is, patients who had become addicted during medical treatment with a notifiable drug – and 1273 (85%) were of nontherapeutic addicts.
- The epidemiological characteristics of platelet aggregability were established in 958 participants in the Northwick Park Heart Study.

– An analysis was conducted of the major findings of a long-term follow-up study of 3076 subjects who were exposed to viral infections in utero and who at the time of analysis were up to 40 years of age.

– Of 76 patients with lateral epicondylitis, 38 were randomly allocated to receive ultrasound treatment and 38 placebos.

– Dermal nitrate preparations are claimed to be useful in the treatment of angina, as their slow absorption bypassing the liver leads to sustained action. Ten patients with angina were exercised on a treadmill after dermal application of 16.64 mg glyceryl trinitrate or 100 mg isosorbide dinitrate or placebo.

– In this practice, with a family practitioner committee list of 9,726 patients, we use a computer register for recall, screening, morbidity data, audit, and repeat prescribing.

– Although the dignostic scope of computed tomography has widened considerably in recent years, assessment of patients with suspected or known malignant disease remains the major reason for body CI referrals in the United Kingdom. This paper sets out to define important advantages and limits of CT in cancer diagnosis, addressing the topics of primary diagnosis, staging, and patient follow-up.

– This article deals with soft-tissue rheumatism and discusses localized soft-tissue lesions of the lower limb. Principles of therapy will also be considered.

– This report is primarily aimed at doctors without experience in general psychiatry who have to deal with patients who have taken a deliberate overdose of drugs.

– Psoriasis is a chronic relapsing inflammatory skin disease characterized by red plaques covered by silvery scales. In this review we outline some clinical features and discuss recent advances in etiology and treatment.

– Six patients with venous thrombo-embolism were treated with heparin, administered intravenously by a constant infusion pump.

– A postal survey identified 114 infants with biliary atresia (roughly one in 21,000 births).

– The intake of anti-inflammatory drugs by 268 patients with colonic or small bowel perforation or hemorrhage was compared with that by a group of patients, matched for age and sex, with uncomplicated lower bowel disease.

INTRODUCTION

– At a time of increasing concern about illicit importation of heroin into the United Kingdom and about the apparently epidemic nature of the use of heroin by young people, it seemed appropriate to review recent experience of opiate dependence in the United Kingdom.

– A review in 1981 of 17 epidemiological studies found in eight an inverse relation between blood cholesterol values and total cancer mortality, particularly in older men, while in the remaining nine studies there was no relation in men or women.

– Jaundice in an infant of more than two weeks of age associated with yellow urine or alcoholic stools indicates potentially serious hepatobiliary disease. Urgent investigation is essential to prevent complications and identify causes.

– The causes of perforation of the gut below the duodenum, except perforation occurring in association with ischemia, are poorly understood.

– Jamieson et al. stated that, apart from sexually transmitted disease, problems of teenage sexuality stem from pregnancy rather than from sexual behavior.

– Sudden unexplained death is the third largest component of infant mortality after perinatal conditions and congenital anomalies. Much research work is being done in Britain and America to unravel the causes of sudden infant death syndrome.

– There are more than 7,000 new cases of bladder cancer each year in the UK.

– Chronic bronchitis and emphysema remains the commonest cause of time lost at work in Britain, and puts an enormous burden of ill health on British society.

– The elderly patient with a fracture of the proximal femur presents a series of medical and social problems.

– Prescribing is a focal point of contact between doctors and patients, and one indicator of the quality of medical care given.

– Hereditary protein C deficiency has recently been shown to carry a high risk of venous thrombosis and embolism. (1–3)

– Blood glucose control is difficult to assess in patients with unstable type I (insulin dependent) diabetes mellitus.

– The results of surveys of patients have shown that there is a high level of satisfaction with the accessibility of general practitioner services. (1–4)

– Two recent prospective epidemiological studies have reported an association between a low prediagnostic serum selenium concentration and the risk of cancer. (1–2)

– Errors by casualty officers in detecting clinically important abnormalities in X-ray films have been reported to be as high as 2% of all examinations. (1)

– The role of platelets in thrombosis has been the subject of numerous studies for many years, especially over the past two decades. In 1962 Born described a method for studying platelet aggregation that was based on changes in the optical density of suspension of platelets. (1–2)

MATERIALS, SUBJECTS, METHODS, DESIGN

– Each doctor was presented with the full list of drugs prescribed during the 21 days (Table 1) and agreed to take one or two categories and draw up a limited list based on need, economy, and suitability (Table 2).

– The study population of 630 people aged 2–74 was first examined in 1962–63 and consisted of two rural samples and one urban sample of people with at least half-Maori ancestry.

– We used the data of the Eastern Finland Heart Survey 1977, which served as the terminal survey of the North Karelia Project. (34)

– Six patients entering our clinical study unit between February and April 1984 with the diagnosis of venous thrombo-embolism (without massive pulmonary embolism) participated in this study.

– The data were obtained by a postal survey of members of the British Paediatric Association Gastroenterology Group and the British Association of Paediatric Surgeons, the survey having been endorsed by these organizations.

– In 1978, a 27-year-old woman suddenly had three generalized epileptic fits within one hour after one week of diffuse headaches.

– The reference intervals for serum fructosarmine, fasting plasma glucose and HbA1C concentrations were determined in thirty healthy nondiabetic volunteers from the hospital laboratory.

– Patients included in the study fell into four groups.

– The computer program is divided into several parts.

– From August 1982 radiographers marked the envelopes of all casualty radiographs thought to show abnormalities.

– From December 1982 to November 1983 all families whose babies were brought to the accident and emergency department of this hospital with a presumptive diagnosis of the sudden infant death syndrome were included in our study.

RESULTS

– The total number of deaths of addicts during the 15-year study was 1499, and Table 1 shows their annual distribution.

– The 17-year, age-specific mortality patterns were comparable to those observed after 11 years. (7) One-third (33.9%) of the deaths were from cardiovascular disease and one-fifth (20.7%) from cancer, similar to the national mortality patterns. (12)

– The tables show the results. Ninety-three of the radiographers' forms were incomplete, and a further 39 were marked "too busy to complete."

– Table 1 gives clinical details for the six patients studied. During the study one (case 1) sustained mild bleeding (hemoptysis) at the end of the night.

– A total of 114 cases of biliary atresia were reported. Two pediatric surgeons were unable to cooperate in the study.

– The mean pre-follow-up serum selenium concentration of the subjects who died of cancer during follow-up was 53.7 (SE 1.8 µg/l) and that of the controls 60.9 (1.8 µg/l).

– Figure 2 shows the correlations between the four parameters. All the correlations were significant at p = 0.01 at least. Figure 2 shows the relation between aggregability and age.

– Altogether 740 sets of records were extracted using separate ICD codes; Table 1 shows the proportions of patients who were definitely recorded as taking or not taking drugs when admitted.

– Fourteen babies who were victims of the sudden infant death syndrome were brought to this hospital during the study. Our sample showed the unexpected cluster of deaths in the winter months and the expected preponderance of boys over girls (Table 3).

– An analysis of the last 100 cases seen by the social security officer during the past few months showed the following breakdown of inquiries: attendance allowance, four; mobility allowance, six; . . . .

– During the 21-day-period 2336 patients received a prescription, either as a result of direct contact with the doctor (1558 patients) or as a request for a repeat prescription (778 patients).

DISCUSSION

1. *Opening.* The incidence of biliary atresia found in this survey (roughly 0.5/10,000 live births) was lower than in other series (0.8-1.0/10,000 live births) 12–14, suggesting a degree of under-reporting.
1. *Closing.* This survey suggests that a similar approach [to the practice in Japan] in the United Kingdom would increase the number of infants who become free of jaundice after surgery, and may improve the long-term prognosis in biliary atresia.

2. *Opening.* Continuous intravenous administration of heparin did not provide a constant anticoagulant effect in the six patients.
2. *Closing.* We believe that the circadian variation should be taken into account when evaluating the heparin dose to be administered. The time at which blood is taken for coagulation tests appears to be crucial, and the rate of heparin infusion might be adapted according to these biological rhythms. Further studies will be necessary before extrapolating our results to all patients receiving treatment with heparin.

3. *Opening.* Perforation and hemorrhage are occasional and well-described complications of idiopathic ulcerative colitis and Crohn's disease, and perforation may occur in established bowel infarction.
3. *Closing.* We suggest that patients with bowel perforation or hemorrhage are particularly likely to be takers of anti-inflammatory drugs, and that the association may be causal.

4. *Opening.* So far, we have studied 53 patients with hereditary protein C deficiency belonging to 20 unrelated Dutch families.
4. *Closing.* We conclude that cerebral venous infarction due to protein C deficiency should be considered if spontaneous cerebral symptoms occur in young patients, especially if they have a family history of

venous thrombo-embolism.

5. *Opening.* Critical appraisal discloses problems with most of the traditional methods of monitoring blood glucose control in young insulin dependent diabetic patients.

5. *Closing.* We present the fructosamine assay as a practical alternative measure of overall blood glucose control and the efficacy of insulin treatment in insulin dependent diabetics. The test is cheap and simple to perform, using equipment available in most routine service laboratories.

6. *Opening.* There were two major problems in making comparisons between recordings in a control group and those from infants destined to be victims of the sudden infant death syndrome.

6. *Closing.* Our findings suggest that the simplest indices of respiratory rate, respiratory rate variability, heart rate, and heart rate variability, measured over 24 hours, are of little value in discriminating between infants who go on to be victims of the sudden infant death syndrome, and control infants.

7. *Opening.* Our findings confirm that ultrasound enhances recovery in patients with lateral epicondylitis, but in only 63% of cases.

7. *Closing.* Clarke and Stenner (15) and Allen and Battye (16) noted considerable changes in ultrasonic output with time. Using a simple underwater balance, we confirmed these changes in radiation output, emphasizing the need for frequent assessment.

Language Functions in Medical Writing

Scientific writing has a concentration of many types of concepts that have specific functions in English. *Cause* and *result* are concepts that are very important in the description of an experiment or of a patient's symptoms. Just as the start of a medical paper must state the *purpose* of a particular piece of research, so might a conclusion contain certain *recommendations*. Here is a selection of the most important types of language function, with examples of how they are used.

EXPRESSING CAUSE AND RESULT

Causes . . . is caused by . . .
results in/from . . . is the result of . . .
is responsible for . . . gives rise to . . . is due to . . .

A *cause* is something that produces an effect; an event, thing, or person that makes something happen. In order to express causality we can say, for instance, that "X causes Y" or that "Y is caused by X." Cause is linked to the notion of *result*, which is the outcome or effect produced by an activity or cause. We can not only say, therefore, that "X is responsible for (gives rise to, results in) Y" but that "Y is due to X" or that "Y is the result of X" or "Y results from X."

1. Alveolar and airways damage is predominantly a result of cigarette smoking, although environmental air pollution can also be responsible.
2. In interior dislocation of the lens, the pupil is blocked by the lens, causing a secondary glaucoma.
3. Unfortunately, a complication still seen is aseptic bone necrosis caused by excessive steroid therapy.
4. Emphysema gives rise to airways obstruction.
5. Airways obstruction is largely responsible for many of the disabling features of bronchitis and emphysema.
6. Fibrinolytic activity results from the conversion of pre-enzyme plasminogen to the active protoeolytic enzyme plasmin.
7. The procedure may, however, be difficult, and is not without

hazard, as the obstruction invariably increases as soon as the patient lies down; the distress and hypoxia in one such instance resulted in a cardiac arrest.

DEFINING

X is a (definition)
X, a (definition), is (further information)
X is a (definition), which (further information)
A (word) is a (definition)
X may be defined as a (definition)
We can define X as a (definition)

1. The hangman's fracture, a traumatic spondylolisthesis of the axis, so called because the bony damage is similar to that seen in judicial hanging, is produced by extension of the head on the neck, with distraction.
2. AIDS is a viral disease that attacks the body's immune system.
3. Menopause, or the cessation of menses, is an event that can only be defined retrospectively.
4. The neuroleptic malignant syndrome is a life-threatening complication of major tranquilizers that is probably underdiagnosed.
5. The neuroleptic malignant syndrome is an idiosyncratic reaction to neuroleptic drugs characterized by muscular rigidity, hyperthermia, autonomic instability, and altered consciousness, and is often complicated by aspiration pneumonia, esophagitis and acute renal failure.
6. Mobility allowance may be awarded to a disabled person aged between 5 and 65 years if he is unable or "virtually unable" to walk. Everyone understands inability to walk but there is no agreement on what constitutes "virtual" inability to walk. It is difficult to quantify gait in a clinically useful way but . . . .

EXPRESSING POSSIBILITY, LIKELIHOOD, AND CERTAINTY

Note these ways of predicting what will happen:

Possibility

May and *might* are used when you want to say that something is possible. There is no significant difference between these expressions. You can say: "He may be in his office. Take a look," or "He might be in his office. . . ." The negative is *may not* or *might not*. To express possibility in the past you use *may have (done)* or *might have (done)*. Consider this example: "He might have needed further medication . . . but we decided to let the infection run its course."

Other expressions of possibility are *possibly* and *perhaps*, e.g., "Viral infection could possibly be the cause of this man's pyrexia." *Can/could* indicate that situations or events are possible: "Smoking can damage your health."

Likelihood

Likely indicates that something is expected. *Likely* means the same as *probable (probably)*. However, it is used in different structures:

be + likely + infinitive
"The dentist is likely to be late tomorrow."
"I think it's likely to snow tomorrow."

it is likely + that-clause
"I think it's likely that the patient will need a further operation."
"It is unlikely that the results will prove positive."

Certainty

Certainty is the notion that there is *no doubt* about something, that something will *undoubtedly* occur. It is an expression of confidence, and is usually indicated by a group of adverbs: *certainly, definitely, clearly, obviously, probably, really*. It is important to understand the correct position of these adverbs:

be + adverb
"There is clearly an inaccuracy in this case history."

auxiliary verb + adverb
"The blood sample has obviously not arrived yet."

adverb + other verb
"Ms. Wilson certainly looks fresher this morning."

1. An alternative approach might have been to apply a halo brace. This would have been particularly useful since there was no bony displacement.
2. Elderly patients may be more susceptible to the adverse effects of the tricyclics, perhaps due to existing CNS dysfunction or cardiac disease.
3. In some patients, hormonal factors might be involved: the disease may present after pregnancy, or on starting oestrogen-therapy.
4. Some evidence has suggested that certain phase II conjugating enzymes (e.g., glucuronyl transferase) may be induced.
5. There is a good chance that a solution to the problem will be found in the next few years.
6. It may be that the greater decrease in mortality observed in women is consistent with the fact that more women than men are currently receiving (and using) antihypertensive treatment.

7. In the investigation of stains, valuable evidence is likely to be obtained in a high proportion of cases.
8. Stress is certain to be a factor in this man's abdominal pain.
9. It could simply be shingles. We'll have to check this out.
10. There is no doubt that diet plays a role in his poor condition.
11. The drug certainly has no effect on post-herpetic neuralgia.

COMPARING

like   unlike
more than   less than
a great deal more/less than
(not) significantly greater/smaller than
in contrast with
compared to
one . . . another

1. Unlike some drugs, the pill is probably as effective in smokers as it is in nonsmokers.
2. Gamma benzene hexachloride is a great deal less safe than more modern agents, but has been – and still is – widely used without problems.
3. The ANF test is cheap and almost easier to perform than the latex test for rheumatoid arthritis.
4. Rashes are rather more common with Alclofenac than with other propionic acid derivatives.
5. Whichever compound is chosen, one group of patients will improve after a week or two of treatment, and another group will show no response.
6. More doctors than before are now seeing at least some children with head lice.
7. The drug is not as safe as Malathion but has a much faster action.
8. Pentazocine priming and maintenance doses for supplementation of nitrous oxide anesthesia are significantly greater in smokers.
9. In general terms, smokers have lower plasma concentrations of induced drugs, and may require larger doses than nonsmokers to obtain a similar pharmacological effect.
10. This finding is in contrast with a single previous study, which failed to detect urokinase in normal colorectal mucosa.

EXPRESSING PURPOSE

In order to (often when no strong purpose is intended the preposition *to* is used without *in order*. This is seen, for example, after verbs describing drug preparations that are *designed to . . . formulated to . . .* etc.)

1. The aim of this study is to show that in patients with anorexia nervosa peripheral blood leucocyte zinc content reflects the tissue state.
2. The drug is formulated to exert a direct local effect, relieving muscle spasms and associated pain or gaseous distension.
3. The principal physiological role of tissue plasminogen activator is to maintain the vascular tree free of fibrin.
4. In order to determine the extent of this uncertainty, we sent a questionnaire to senior clinicians so as to find out whether there might be a genetic predisposition to depression or other psychiatric disorders among adolescent suicides. A study was conducted by . . . .
5. Determination of ratios of HDL to LDL have been advocated in order to establish markers of the risk of coronary heart disease in patients with excess LDL cholesterol.
6. The purpose of this report is to show that, whereas this agent is designed to act locally on intestinal smooth muscle, it is not free from anticholinergic side effects.
7. An aliquot was removed in order to measure plasma zinc and albumin concentrations.
8. The capsule is designed to pass through the stomach intact, allowing the active ingredient, peppermint oil, to reach the usual source of these symptoms – the colon.
9. The meeting was postponed until 3 o'clock so that all the staff could attend.
10. The role of the new unit is to supplement existing psychiatric facilities.

USING THE PASSIVE

The *passive* is a verb phrase that uses the construction *be* + participle, or it may be a clause in which a passive verb phrase occurs. The opposite of passive is active. Notice that the large majority of passive clauses do not require the *by* phrase. This is particularly true of scientific and official writing. The matter of who performs an action is often unimportant. For example, in the sentence: "A vagotomy was performed," it is irrelevant to state that the operation was performed by a surgeon unless you specially want to point out that it was Mr. McGregor (and not Mr. Turnbull) that performed the operation.

1. On admission to hospital he was disoriented and cyanosed and was thought to be suffering from bronchopneumonia.
2. A 47-year-old housewife was referred to the dermatology clinic.
3. There is no evidence of a specific skin disease, so a systemic cause is suggested.

4. In the early stages, bile duct damage is shown by swelling.
5. Aziaprine is being evaluated in a controlled trial.
6. Pruritus can be treated with cholestyramine.
7. Supplements of fat-soluble vitamins and calcium should be given immediately.
8. He had been told he suffered from renal stones and had been hospitalized on two occasions in Detroit.
9. While in the coronary unit his hematuria was noted to have disappeared.
10. The infective agent has not yet been isolated.
11. Her leukemia had been discovered after a routine blood count prior to her hysterectomy for fibroids.
12. A careful history and clinical examination, including a rectal examination and sigmoidoscopy, can be performed by the general practitioner, and the cause of bleeding elicited in most cases there and then.
13. Hemorrhoids are undoubtedly the commonest cause of this symptom, and these, too, can be treated in the surgery by injection therapy. The technique will be described in a subsequent article in this journal.
14. The patient is advised to have the bowels well open before attending for sigmoidoscopy.
15. Dental extractions are always accompanied by a bacteremia.

EXPRESSING OBLIGATION

In order to express the idea of obligation, to talk about rules, duties, or orders, to give strong advice to other people or to ourselves we use *must, have (got) to, should,* and *ought to. Should* and *ought to* have the same meaning. They are used when a speaker thinks it is a good thing or right that a person does something. It indicates that a person has a duty to do something.

"You really should stop smoking."

"Patients ought to stop smoking in the waiting room."

Must is used to order someone (or oneself) to do something, while *have to* means that there is a rule that forces that person to do something (see Expressing Necessity, p. 46). Consider these examples:

"I really must contact Dr. Phillips today."

"You have to fill out this form before coming."

1. Investigations should include plain skull X-rays, audiometry and caloric testing.
2. Blood cultures should also be done to exclude an associated septicemia.
3. Syphilis serology should be carried out in all patients suffering from neurological disease, and, in this case, a Paul-Bunnell and

titer for B virus should be performed.

4. In this case, the high pulse rate should have alerted the obstetrician to the potential hazard that could be encountered with a beta-stimulant drug, and Salbutamol should not have been given.

5. The patient should be treated with dexamethasone, a synacthen stimulation test should be performed, and adrenal antibodies should be sought.

6. Many doctors believe that any patient with sinusitis ought to have a sinus X-ray.

7. Particular care should be taken when tailing off steroids after they have been given for some time, even in low dosage.

8. Two of the drugs that should be used with caution are tetracycline and co-trimoxazole.

9. If one drug does not work another should be tried, and if necessary ECT should be considered.

10. If heart failure is mild, treatment ought to be commenced with potassium supplements and a thiazide diuretic.

11. Steroids should be given for two years and then withdrawn with a careful watch for relapse.

12. All sores should be swabbed, but antibiotics are only used if a surrounding cellulitis is present.

RECOMMENDING

is (not) recommended
it would seem wise to . . .   it might be wise to . . .
is (are) best + past participle
it is advisable . . .   it might be advisable to . . .

1. It would seem wise to avoid the use of estrogen-containing oral contraceptive agents in patients with prolactinomas who are receiving bromocriptine.

2. All patients who have suffered a TIA or minor stroke are best helped to stop smoking as soon as possible.

3. It is recommended that reserve supplies of ampicillin, amoxycillin, and trimethoprim be provided for the patient to use when necessary.

4. Oral long-acting theophylline derivatives are best taken in the evening to combat nocturnal breathlessness.

5. Intravenous preparations are best given slowly to avoid fatal arrhythmias.

6. This booster antihypertensive is not recommended for the treatment of children under the age of twelve years, since safe conditions for its use have not been established.

7. In these circumstances, it would be advisable to leave the

catheters *in situ* for up to two weeks.
8. Rectal absorption of narcotics is slow and irregular. It might be advisable, therefore, to supplement oral therapy last thing at night and to prevent early reawakening from pain.
9. Phenazocine is particularly useful in this context, and more recently buprenorphine has been recommended.

EXPRESSING NECESSITY

We use *must* and *have to* (do) or simply *need to* when we want to say that it is necessary to do something. These expressions are generally interchangeable, e.g., "I need to telephone Nurse Kendall/I must telephone Nurse Kendall/I have to telephone Nurse Kendall." There is sometimes a difference, however, between *must* and *have to*. With *must* there is some expression of personal feeling involved. The writer (or speaker) feels that something is necessary. Consider this example:

"The Health Minister really must solve the problem of the shortage of beds in the city."

On the other hand, *have to* is used to present the facts – not to express strong views, opinions, or personal feelings.

"I have to visit out-patients next week."

"I have to attend a meeting next Monday, so we'll have to arrange another time to discuss this."

As well as *need to* there is also the expression *necessary*. This is used with the verb *be* as in the following example:

"It may be necessary to transfuse this patient."

"It is clearly not necessary to increase the dosage."

1. The patient felt she had to seek psychiatric help.
2. Leukemia has to be excluded, and investigations should therefore include a blood film and marrow examination.
3. This man must be further investigated with sputum cytology, and, if necessary, following his recovery, bronchoscopy.
4. Urea and electrolytes and liver function test estimation are helpful but it must be remembered that up to two-thirds of renal function may be lost before the blood urea begins to rise.
5. Once a diuresis is started it is often maintained with oral therapy, and care has to be taken not to over-diurese and dehydrate the patient.
6. Treatment is the same as for younger age groups, but more care must be taken as the risk of side effects is greater.
7. Some commonly used drugs are known to aggravate epilepsy and their concurrent use must be avoided.
8. The patient had to wait three months for the operation.
9. When used for pain control in terminal care an adequate dose needs to be given to alleviate pain at all times.

10. The burden of washing soiled sheets, especially daily, and also having to cope with wet or dirty clothes can often be the last straw for the caring relative.
11. The patient had to work nights and his sexual activity was severely restricted.
12. A decision to withhold or withdraw treatment for terminally ill patients does not mean that symptomatic relief has to be abandoned.
13. Alcoholic neuropathy must be considered as a possible diagnosis in this case.
14. Investigations must be aimed at finding an etiological agent.
15. Investigations must delineate if there is an obstruction to her biliary tract.
16. The results obtained from electrophysiological methods of investigation must always be considered in relation to the clinical features of the patient.

MAKING GENERALIZATIONS

tend   is a tendency to/toward
incline   is inclined to
seems   on the whole   by and large
generally
in the majority of cases

1. There seems, on the whole, no commonly agreed mode of treatment for atrial fibrillation.
2. GPs have been inclined to overlook the problem of poor housing.
3. In the vast majority of cases there was no sign of anemia.
4. It has become generally accepted that change must take place.
5. There is, by and large, no general agreement on the best way to define mild to moderate hypertension.
6. Such patients tend not to be persuaded by assertions that self-treatment with cod liver oil for this condition is useless.
7. These symptoms are inclined to reappear after a period of 3–4 months.

GIVING EMPHASIS

The *do* structures (*do, does, did*) are often used to give emphasis to the following verb. For example:

"Do sit down."
"The meeting did seem rather long."

Another way of emphasizing important information in a sentence is by using special structures such as the following.

What (+ subject) + verb + be

"What the doctor must recognize is the danger of mistakenly passing the tube into the esophagus and thereby, most likely, killing the patient."

"What is essential is that past studies on AIDS in nonhuman primates (simian T lymphotropic virus types I and III) be taken into account, when studying their human counterpart virus."

A writer can also emphasize an idea by using the structure *It is/was . . . that . . . .* For example:

"It was the presence of asbestos in the roof that made us suspect poisoning."

"It is the lack of family support that exacerbates the problem."

1. Infection is probably less important, although it does increase morbidity and mortality in patients with gross lung disease.
2. There was a very low uptake of rehabilitation services by the families. Nevertheless, a few families did attend the self-help organization *Headway* for relatives of victims of severe head injury.
3. This approach to treatment does certainly have the advantage of preventing any serious fall in plasma level.
4. These Slow-K preparations do seem to be a genuine pharmaceutical advance, and problems occur only if the tablets become impacted.
5. Management of this particular type of patient does require special skills.
6. What I am most concerned about in this NHS debate is the apparent obsession with a monetary solution to a problem that requires understanding and generosity.
7. It is the problem of retrosternal symptoms that has caused the patient most concern.
8. What I am dubious about is the statement that "more money is the solution to the problems of the shortage of beds."

Avoiding Sexism in Medical Writing

More and more medical journals are becoming sensitive to the need to modify implied or irrelevant evaluation of the sexes, for example, "man and wife" instead of the more correct "husband and wife." It is useful, therefore, to be aware of this fact when writing in English.

The purpose of this section is to show how modern scientific writers try to avoid what is called "sexism" in writing by making word choices that do not imply sex differences when no such differences are warranted, e.g., overuse of the pronoun *he* when *she* or *they* would be equally appropriate. Or, alternatively, sexism may involve making generalizations about all people from one sex.

The conscious effort to minimize the long-established cultural practice of sexism in language need not lead to awkwardness or obscurity. Some medical journals provide guidelines to aid writers in this matter. Check the style sheet of the particular journal if you are thinking of contributing an article. With attention to meaning and careful rephrasing, writing in English can become more accurate and unbiased. Consider the following ways in which you can modify stereotyped language in writing and speaking:

Common usage	Action	Suggested change
mankind, man	Substitute variety of terms.	humanity, human beings, people, the human species
the average man	Substitute variety of terms.	the average person, people in general
manpower	Substitute variety of terms.	staffing, personnel, the workforce
The doctor . . . he . . .	Change to pl.	Doctors . . . they . . .
The student . . . he . . .	Change to pl.	Students . . . they . . .
The dentist . . . he . . .	Change to pl.	Dentists . . . they . . .
The nurse . . . she . . .	Change to pl.	Nurses . . . they . . .

49

Common usage	Action	Suggested change
Each patient was receiving transfusions every 14–21 days in an effort to maintain his hemoglobin concentrations greater than 100g/l.	Delete *his*. Introduce plural.	All patients were receiving transfusions every 14–21 days in an effort to maintain hemoglobin concentrations. . . .
The group comprised 7 school refusals (4 boys and 3 girls). Each person was asked to write down in his own diary	Introduce plural.	The study group comprised 7 school refusals (4 boys and 3 girls). They were asked to write down in their diaries . . . .
Student performance was measured by the difference between his expected score and his actual score.	Delete *his*. Introduce article *the*.	Student performance was measured by the difference between the expected score and the actual score.
The individual is essentially alone but the trauma of a bereavement makes his loneliness real and his environment hostile.	Replace *his* with pronoun and article – *our* and *the*.	The individual is essentially alone but the trauma of a bereavement makes our loneliness real and the environment hostile.
Woman doctor	Omit sex reference unless necessary.	Doctor, physician
Male nurse	Omit sex reference unless necessary.	Nurse
Chairman (of meeting)	Substitute alternative nouns.	Chair, Chairperson
Foreman	Substitute alternative nouns.	Supervisor
Policeman	Substitute alternative nouns.	Police officer
Doctors do not always, however, promote basic health awareness among their wives and children.	Choose wording to acknowledge that women as well as men are doctors.	Doctors do not always, however, promote basic health awareness among their spouses and children.

Writing Letters and Notes

A letter is the representative of the writer. It may take the form of a simple message or request, or it might convey extensive and complex information. In either case it may need to convey (in the case of formal letters) the professional standing of the writer by its appearance as well as by its content. In this section, a selection of model letters, brief notes, and telexes are displayed. It is useful to remember that in modern letter-writing there is much variation in the style of presentation. Also, while there are differences in style between British and North American letters there is overlapping and one can sometimes see a transatlantic blending and variety of styles. Here are some general guidelines that can be referred to when writing letters.

The Letter-heading

Write your address at the top of the letter in the right-hand corner. The house number is written first, then the street name, then the town. There are usually punctuation marks in the address.

The Date

The date appears under the address. There are several ways of writing the date. In the United States and other countries the figure for the month comes first: 5.26.94 (26th May 1994). In Britain this would be written 26.5.94. Other ways of writing the date are:

May 5th 1994 or 5 May 1994 or May 5, 1994

Notice that, in speaking, British usage for 5 May 1994 is "May the fifth, nineteen ninety-four" *or* "The fifth of May, nineteen ninety-four"; whereas the North American usage is "May fifth, nineteen-ninety-four."

The Addressee

The title, name, and address of the person you are writing to are written on the left side of the page. The first line is placed either on the same level, or, more usually, just below the level of the date.

Typewritten Addresses

Addresses may be "blocked," with each line flush with the left margin, or indented, so that each line is moved several spaces to the right of the one above. Indenting is less common; the blocked style is neater, quicker, and more modern. Commas are optional, but secretaries will often intentionally leave them out. At all events, it is better to be consistent.

The Greeting

The letter begins on the left side of the page with *Dear*. In formal letters you write the name of the addressee with the appropriate title. For example: Mr. Day, Ms. (Mrs. or Miss) Fellowes. American usage places a period (full stop) after Dr., Mr., Mrs., or Ms., while in Britain it is omitted.

If a letter happens to be addressed to more than one person, then the plural form is attached to the title, as in:

Dear Professors Ulrich and Lin-Po,
Dear Messrs. Howden,
Dear Mesdames Nishizono,

Or alternatively:

Dear Professor Ulrich and Professor Lin-Po,

Sometimes a combination of titles is required when writing to two people as in the following examples:

Dear Dr. and Mr. Yeliseyeva,
Dear Dr. and Mrs. Young,

A comma or colon is placed after the greeting.

The Letter-ending

Ending a letter depends on what the form of greeting was. If you begin with *Dear Sir(s)* or *Dear Madam* it is usual to finish with *Yours faithfully*. This is appropriate, therefore, when the name of the addressee is not known. If you begin with the person's name, as in *Dear Dr. Wilson,* the letter may finish with *Yours sincerely*. In the case of informal letters, such as letters to friends, in which the first name only has been used, it is customary to finish with an expression like *Yours* or *Love*. We can put this in the following table:

Formal Letters

Addressee unknown	Greeting	Ending
The Superintendent	Dear Sir or Madam,	Yours faithfully,
Addressee known		
Dr. Koh	Dear Dr. Koh,	Yours sincerely,
		Sincerely yours,
		Sincerely,

Informal Letters

Addressee known		
Dr. Parker	Dear Bill,	Yours,
Dr. Wall	Dear Jane,	Love,

The Envelope

On the envelope the title, name, and surname are placed on the first line in
that order. *Mr.* is used for men who do not have another title. *Miss* is used
for unmarried women or young girls and *Mrs.* for married women. The title
Ms. (pronounced "Miz") is becoming increasingly preferred by some
women and is used when the addressee's status, i.e., married or unmarried,
is not relevant, e.g., *Ms.* Baker, *Ms.* Rowe.

The usual form of writing the address is as follows:

1. House number/street name	1 S. Fourth Avenue
2. Name of city	Ann Arbor
3. Name of county or state	Michigan
4. Postcode (Britain) or Zip code (USA)	48109
5. Country	U.S.A.

British and Canadian postcodes are a combination of letters and
numbers. An Edinburgh (Scottish) postcode may be EH9 lJB whereas the
zip (Zone Improvement Plan) code is a five-digit number placed after the
name of the state, e.g., AZ 86011 (Arizona).

Some envelopes bear the sender's name and address in the top left-hand
corner. Alternatively, it is possible to type/write your name and address on
the back of the envelope. Customs vary from country to country and there
seems to be no hard-and-fast rule. It is best to do as you think appropriate.

There may be some doubt in the sender's mind as to whether or not the
addressee has moved to another address. Many people now make arrangements with their post office to forward mail. Just to make certain that letters
will be sent on it is possible to write in the top left-hand corner or top
middle: PLEASE FORWARD.

If it is very important for the sender to know whether the letter has
reached its proper destination you can take the precaution of writing in the
top left-hand corner: IF UNDELIVERED PLEASE RETURN TO (Name
+ Address). (Most undelivered mail will be returned anyway.)

A fairly common category of letter in the professional/academic world
is the *letter of introduction,* in which, for example, a foreign student Ms.
Maruta goes to study in the laboratory of Professor Schmidt in Minnesota,
who is a friend of Professor Kono in Osaka. Professor Kono may write a
letter of introduction for Ms. Maruta and write in the top left-hand corner
of the envelope: "Introducing Ms. Keiko Maruta."

SAMPLE LETTERS

Requesting Information

Department of Psychiatry.
Fukuoka University,
Nanakuma 34, Nishi-ku,
Tokyo,
JAPAN.

23rd July 1990

The Secretary,
Royal Edinburgh Hospital,
Morningside Place,
EDINBURGH EH 10.

Dear Sir/Madam,

Would you kindly send me details of the forthcoming International Conference on Adolescent Psychiatry to be held at the Royal Edinburgh Hospital in June, 1991?

Yours faithfully,

Akiko Nishikawa, M.D.

Application for Study

Department of Oncology,
Beijing Medical College,
Beijing,
People's Republic of China.

September 4, 1991

The Secretary,
Department of Radiology,
University of Leeds,
Woodhouse Lane,
Leeds, LS 1,
ENGLAND.

Dear Sir or Madam,

I would be grateful if you could send me information about postgraduate study in the Department of Radiology. I am a Chinese doctor with a medical degree from the University of Shanghai, and with 9 years' clinical experience at a city hospital, including work in the Department of Radiology.

I should be grateful for your advice on the facilities for M.Phil. or Ph.D. study in your department, and, if my application proves to be successful, when might be a suitable time to come to England?

Yours faithfully,

Wang Lung-yin (Dr)

Subscribing to a Journal

                                        Division of Sexually
                                        Transmitted Diseases,
                                        Clinical Research Center,
                                        Xiao, China.

                                        December 4, 1993.

Subscription Manager,
British Medical Journal,
BMA House,
Tavistock Square,
London WC1H 9JR.

Dear Sir,

I would like to take out a subscription to the British
Medical Journal. Would you kindly send me the
appropriate details?

Yours faithfully,

Wang Ping, M.D.

Letter of Acknowledgment

16, Rue de Descartes,
Montmartre,
Paris.

August 10, 1992

Professor Shuzo Yamamoto,
Institute of Dermatology,
University of Newcastle,
Blaydon St., Newcastle,
ENGLAND.

Dear Professor Yamamoto,

Thank you very much for accepting me for your summer
course in dermatology. I heard yesterday from my
superiors that they are willing to sponsor me. I shall
be arriving in Newcastle on June 28th and will contact
your department directly.

Yours sincerely,

Sylvie Mulphin, M.D.

Letter of Welcome

July 11, 1993

Professor Jinda Napapon
Dept. of Pathology
Chiang Mai Medical College
Chiang Mai, Thailand

Dear Professor Napapon

We are delighted that you are able to join us here in Michigan.

I have contacted the University Accommodation Officer who will be writing to you in the immediate future. It is likely that you will be staying in the North University apartment complex. We need to know immediately whether you will be accompanied by your husband and children. Also, will you need any help with your visa?

I look forward to your visit and to hearing about the work which you are doing in Chiang Mai.

Yours sincerely,

Brian Rolyan M.D., Ph.D.

Letter of Introduction

Department of Public Health,
School of Medicine,
University of Queensland,
South Brisbane 4101,
Australia.

January 5th, 1995.

The Medical Library,
University of Wisconsin,
Madison, W1 53706,
U.S.A.

Dear Sir or Madam,

Mr John Sasagawa who brings this letter to you is a graduate student in the School of Medicine, at the University of Queensland. He intends to spend a few days in Madison and would like to take the opportunity of visiting your library. I would appreciate it if you would give him your co-operation.

Yours sincerely,

Utako Stevenson, MD
Professor and Chairperson
Department of Public Health

Letter of Introduction

University College, London

7 The Maltings
Gower Place
London   WC1 2E

July 5 1993

Professor William Halstead
Department of Social Psychiatry
University of New South Wales
Arlington, Australia

Dear Bill,

It was good to see you again last April in Paris. Hope
you managed to get all your shopping done before you
left for Rome.

By now you will have met Alan Kim. He has been working
in our lab. for about 3 years now and I commend him to
you as a very hard-working and reliable young man. His
elder sister, by the way, is Nancy Kim the well-known
child psychologist. You will have received further
details about Alan in the CV which he sent earlier. I
am sure he will be an asset to your laboratory during
the short time that he will be with you.

Look forward to seeing you - at the London conference
perhaps?

Best wishes.

Adrian Bolland

Letter of Reference

Department of Psychiatry
Baylor College of Medicine
1 Baylor Plaza
Houston, TX 77030
USA

August 5, 1996

The Simon Medical Foundation
University of Karachi
P.O. Box 8403
Karachi-32
PAKISTAN

Re: Timothy Sands
     Assistant Professor
     Baylor College of Medicine

Dear Professor Quarani

Thank you for your letter of July 1st in which you requested
a brief reference regarding Professor Sands. I am happy
to commend him to your University.

During the time of his appointment in the Department of
Psychiatry (1992-) he has been a stimulating and
valuable member of our team. His clinical skills in
Psychiatry were soon evident from the moment of his
inception in university hospital. After a year's fellowship in psychiatry in Edinburgh his skills in psychiatry
made him the obvious person to assume the newly created
combined post of clinical psychiatrist and Director of
the Young Persons' Unit in 1994. He soon built up a
local and regional service in adolescent psychiatry,
while taking his full share in the clinical practice of
general psychiatry.

In spite of a severe illness in 1995, from which he has
now recovered, his strength of character truly showed
itself, and his colleagues have been impressed at his
cheerful uncomplaining persistence in adversity. He is
a hard-working and reliable member of this university
whom I have no difficulty in recommending to you.

Yours sincerely,

David Reece, MD, PhD
Professor and Chairman
Department of Psychiatry

Request for Reprint of Article

Sheffield Institute of Dermatology,
Long Holton,
Sheffield, SD 16 HY9

10.8.94

Professor S. Taylor,
Department of Dermatology,
Charing Cross Hospital,
London, W6 8RF.

Dear Professor Taylor,

I should greatly appreciate a reprint of your paper:

The state of dermatological research 1980-1990, Journal of
Dermatology, 7 (1990), pp.206-230.

Thank you for your courtesy.

Yours sincerely,

James Norton, Ph.D.

Letter of Thanks for Hospitality

University Department of Medicine
Glasgow Royal Infirmary
Glasgow G40SF
Scotland

5.9.94

First Department of Orthopaedics
Athens University
Athens 115 27
Greece

Dear Dr Messaritakis

On behalf of myself and my colleagues I would like to
extend my thanks to you and your staff during our recent
visit to your department. We were greatly impressed by
all that we saw and enjoyed our discussions with you
during our too brief stay.

It would be a great pleasure to show you our facilities
here in Glasgow. Should you or any of your colleagues
have the occasion to visit Scotland we would be delighted
to show you our new orthopaedics unit.

Once again, thank you for your gracious hospitality.

Yours sincerely,

Eric Glynn
Professor of Orthopaedics

Visiting a Hospital

                                        McGill University
                                        Department of Surgery
                                        Montreal
                                        Quebec 7000
                                        Canada
                                        Telephone (23)345876

                                        January 22, 1998

Dr Thomas Kilroy
Birmingham Maternity Hospital
Birmingham B15 2TB
ENGLAND

Dear Dr Kilroy

I am arranging a visit to England to discuss research
topics in the area of congenital heart disease. I was
most interested in your paper on the genetic epidemiology
of congenital heart disease. Here at McGill we have just
completed a study of the risks to the offspring of
parents operated upon for cardiovascular malformations.

I would be very glad to receive any further information
on your Birmingham study, and, if it is convenient, I
would like to arrange a visit to your unit.

Yours sincerely,

Jeanne D'Artaud
Professor of Surgery

Letter of Referral

Dear Dr O'Reagan,

Re: Mr Neil Munroe   Age: 40 yrs
     71 Stafford Street
     Edinburgh   EH1

This semi-professional guitarist complains of nausea and
headache after sitting for long periods during music tuition.
He also complains of severe low back pain radiating to right
leg. Not relieved by analgesics. Nausea and headache
unrelated to food intake. Bowels and micturition normal.
Unable to sleep. Depressed. Weight loss of 5 kg in the last
5 weeks. Eyesight normal although he has also complained
of eye-strain when reading. Abdomen N.A.D.

Thank you for seeing him.

Yours sincerely,

Dr Peter Weintraub

Letter of Referral Acknowledgment (Consultant to G.P.)

Dear Dr Thyme,

Re: Ms W. McCutcheon,
     45 Roseneath Place,
     Edinburgh EH9

Thank you for sending your patient to see me. I was able
to confirm the presence of pregnancy by both abdominal
and vaginal examination and agree that the size is compatible
with approximately 14 weeks' pregnancy. We have booked her
for delivery in this hospital.

Yours sincerely,

J. Milton
Consultant Gynaecologist

Dear Dr Allan,

Re: Mr A. Burton
     12 Rhodes Lane
     York Y45

Thank you for accepting this patient as arranged by
telephone. This man has been complaining of severe
depression following the death of his wife 14 months
ago. He has also complained of insomnia and a vague
discomfort in the left side of his abdomen. This is
not related to food intake.

I should be glad to have your opinion of him.

Yours sincerely,

James Chan

SAMPLE NOTES

Arranging an Appointment

Dear Professor Bay,

I wonder if I might have a word with you about my proposal for the Ph.D.? Would you kindly let me know when would be convenient? I am free every morning except Friday.

Yours sincerely,

Bang-Yoon

Postponing an Appointment

Dear Dr Kim,

I regret that I must postpone my appointment with you on Thursday. Unfortunately, I have some urgent business at the University regarding my accommodation. May we arrange another day?

Yours sincerely,

Francis Glasser

Taking a Telephone Message

Dr Hamid,

Dr Yeshova called at 11.30 a.m. She would like to contact you regarding tomorrow's appointment. Could you call her on Ext.678 between 2 and 8 p.m.

Alan Jones

Returning Something Borrowed from a Colleague

Dear Stephane,

Many thanks for the report. Very interesting. I'd like to discuss it with you sometime. Where might I be able to get a copy?

Gillian Lefevre

Cards and Greetings

Sometimes it is not necessary to write a letter to a friend or colleague. You can write a postcard, greeting card, or something in the form of a short note.

Postcards

When you are sending a postcard to friends or colleagues at work, there is not much space, so you must keep it short. It is common to leave out some verbs, personal pronouns (I/you/he/she) and the articles (a/the). You can also abbreviate some words, especially *and* (&), *very* (v.), and your initials (JM) if you are well known to your correspondent.

```
15. 8. 91

City much bigger than
expected. V. hot 40°C.
Delicious food. Delightful        Ms. Jane Sasae
place to spend a holiday.         5 Milton Road
  See you on Tuesday.             Highgate
     Best wishes                  London N6
        John M.                    ENGLAND
```

Other phrases for vacation postcards: Having a wonderful time/The city is full of fascinating places/Arrived safely/Have taken lots of photos/The weather is very wet and windy/Soaring temperatures every day/Very bumpy flight/Learning to speak Greek/Seafood mouth-watering/The week's going too fast.

Holiday Cards

Many people only write to acquaintances during the winter holiday season. They include all sorts of interesting information about events of the previous year. Here is an example:

Hope you are well.
I'm now working in the
Central Hospital (Portland,
Oregon). Return to Sweden
in March. Looking forward
to hearing from you.
John

Portland. Dec. 18.
16 Roseneath St.
Portland. OR 48109

Best Wishes for
Christmas
and the
New year

Other phrases for holiday cards: Season's Greetings/Thinking of you this Christmas/Best wishes for Christmas and the New Year/ Have a beautiful Christmas/Happy Hanukkah/See you in the New Year/With warmest greetings for the holidays and the New Year/Merry Christmas and a Happy New Year/With very best wishes.

Reserving a Room at a Hotel

Dear Sir or Madam,

I would be grateful if you would reserve a double room for me (with bathroom or shower) from 11th-16th July inclusive. My wife and I will be arriving sometime in the early evening. Please confirm this booking.

Yours faithfully,

Lasse Peterson   (Dr)

Booking a Flight

Dear Sir or Madam,

I would like to fly from Dusseldorf to London on 3rd February or as early as possible that week.   Would you kindly reserve a seat for me (one-way).

Sincerely yours

Joan Lee-Wang

Seeking Information about Travel, Hotels, etc.

Dear Sir,

I intend to visit Montreal this Fall.   Would you kindly send me information about transport, hotels, and places of interest in the vicinity?

Yours faithfully,

Maria Pavesi

Curriculum Vitae

The curriculum vitae or "Résumé," as it is often called, is a summary or outline of your educational and professional background. It also contains a small amount of personal information, such as your date of birth and addresses (personal and work).

The layout of a typical curriculum vitae is not absolutely fixed. There is variation. However, the essential details should be included. When applying for jobs, you may find that employers will provide you with a blank form to be filled in with various details. This may be instead of or supplementary to your own curriculum vitae. Whatever the organization of your curriculum vitae, it must contain important information such as:

1. Name
2. Address (personal and work)
3. Telephone numbers
4. Date of birth
5. Professional interests
6. Current position/employment
7. Educational background
8. Professional experience
9. Publications in journals, bulletins, or books
   (This should include any postgraduate thesis.)
10. Papers delivered at conferences.

Additional information may be required, such as names and addresses of persons who can be contacted if a reference becomes necessary. Your potential employer will often indicate automatically that these and other important details must be included in your initial application. It is important to remember to include an accompanying letter with the curriculum vitae.

SAMPLE CURRICULUM VITAE

CURRICULUM VITAE

DAVID
YAMASHITA

M.B. Ch.B. (UNIVERSITY OF LIVERPOOL)

MEMBER OF THE ROYAL COLLEGE OF PSYCHIATRISTS

David Yamashita
High Row Hospital
Menston
Yorkshire
England

David Christopher Yamashita

Address: Department of Psychiatry, High Row General
                 Hospital, 145 Mains Drive, Menston,
                 Yorkshire

Home: 16 West Nicolson Street (3rd Floor Left),
                 Ilkley, IK 45L, Yorkshire

Telephone: (0533) 6002341

Date of Birth: 22 February 1948

Nationality: British

Marital Status: Single

Place of Birth: Los Angeles, California, USA

Professional Interests

Adolescent Psychiatry: Psychopathological theory of
                         childhood disturbance; Attachment
                         theory; Interactional theory.

Psychotherapy: Outpatient group psychotherapy;
                         marital therapy; family therapy.

Current Position

Senior Registrar   Department of Psychiatry, High Row
                         Hospital

Education

Membership: Royal College of Psychiatrists 1981

Certificate: Child Psychiatry, Tavistock Clinic 1978

M.D.:   University of Leeds 1975

M.B. CH.B.: University of Liverpool 1972

Professional Experience

Senior Registrar, Psychiatry, High Row Hospital 1981-

Registrar, General Psychiatry, Elm Park Hospital 1978-1981

Senior House Officer, Psychiatry, Jones Memorial Hospital
    1976-19

Publications

Reliability of psychiatric diagnosis: a review of the
    literature Clinical Studies in Psychiatry, vol.4,
    No.3, 1990.

Covert sensitisation. Bulletin of the British Psychological
    Association, vol.45, No.5, 1989.

Cognitive disorder among the schizophrenias, Behaviour
    Research and Therapy, 5. 1988.

Papers Delivered at Conferences

Towards a New Theory of Childhood Disturbance. BAP Conference.
    Edinburgh, 1990.

Essentials of Implosive Theory in Adolescent Psychiatry.
    Yorkshire Psychiatry Association Conference, Leeds, 1989.

A Study of Encounter Group Casualties. British Society of
    Family Therapy. Cardiff, 1988.

Spelling It Right

Watch out for words that may cause confusion because they look and sound alike even though their meaning, spelling, and pronunciation may be different.

ARMS (limbs, weapons)   ALMS (charity)
AURAL (understanding by ear)   ORAL (by mouth)
BALD (alopecia)   BALLED (clenched, e.g., fist)
BARE (naked)   BEAR (carry)
BASE (lowest part)   BASS (voice)
BORN (brought forth)   BORNE (carried)
BLOCK (stop, e.g., heart block)   BLOC (political alliance)
BREAK (destroy)   BRAKE (stop)
BURY (put in ground)   BERRY (type of fruit)
CELL (unity of matter, e.g., blood cell)   SELL (exchange for money)
CHECK (investigate)   CHEQUE (money/British)
CORD (string, e.g., spinal cord)   CHORD (in music)
CORE (center)   CORPS (section of army)
COARSE (rough, e.g., coarse skin)   COURSE (program)
DISGUST (ill feeling)   DISCUSSED (debated)
DIE (cease to exist)   DYE (staining agent)
FAINT (lose consciousness, indistinct)   FEINT (pretend)
FISSURE (split, e.g., anal fissure)   FISHER (catcher of fish)
FLU (influenza)   FLEW (past tense of *fly*)   FLUE (inside of chimney)
GAIT (way of walking)   GATE (entrance)
GNAW (eat, e.g., gnawing pain)   NOR (neither . . . nor)
GROAN (low exclamation of pain)   GROWN (past tense of *grow*)
HEAL (cure)   HEEL (back part of foot)
HOARSE (rough voice, e.g., after sore throat)   HORSE (animal)
ION (electrically charged particle)   IRON (type of metal, Fe)
LARVA (embryo of animal)   LAVA (discharge from volcano)
LESSEN (decrease)   LESSON (learning experience)
LUMBAR (spinal region)   LUMBER (wood, timber)
MOAN (exclamation of pain, complaint)   MOWN (cut, past tense of *mow*)
MOULD (fungi, e.g., penicillin/British)   MOULD (to shape, model substance/British)
MOLD (fungi, e.g., penicillin/U.S.)   MOLD (to shape, model substance/U.S.)
MUSCLE (body tissue)   MUSSEL (type of shellfish)
MIND (mentality, memory, thought)   MINED (past tense of *mine*; to dig)
MUCUS (secretion of mucosa)   MUCOUS (adjective from *mucus*)
NAVEL (umbilical)   NAVAL (adjective from *navy*)
PAIN (suffering)   PANE (glass of window)

75

PATIENTS (patients under medical treatment)   PATIENCE (calm endurance)
PEACE (quiet, absence of suffering)   PIECE (portion)
PITTED (holed, e.g., pitted skin)   PITIED (past tense of *pity*)
POTION (medicinal dose)   PORTION (part)
RIGOR (body rigidity on death)   RIGOR/RIGOUR (thoroughness)
RETCH (vomit)   WRETCH (unfortunate person)
RHEUM (rheumatic, rheumatoid)   ROOM (enclosed space)
SICK (ill, vomit)   SIC (device for ascribing error)
SIGHT (vision)   CITE (quote)   SITE (position)
STARE (gaze fixedly)   STAIR (steps in building)
STYE (eyelid abscess)   STY (pig's dwelling)
SKULL (cranium)   SCULL (oar, type of boat)
SLOUGH (to shed skin)   SLOUGH (marshy area)
SORE (painful, skin eruption)   SAW (past tense of *see*)   SOAR (to rise high)
STANCH (to stop bleeding, e.g., tourniquet)   STAUNCH (loyal support)
SWAB (surgical drying material)   SLOB (rude, aggressive person)
TEAR (secretion of lachrymal gland)   TIER (row, rank, layer)
TIC (muscular twitch)   TICK (parasitic insect)
TIRE (to lack energy)   TIRE/TYRE (rubber part of wheel)
TOE (metatarsus)   TOW (to pull boat, car, etc.)
VEIN (blood-vessel)   VAIN (useless; conceited)   VANE (flag, weathercock)
VIAL (small flask for medicine)   VIOL (musical instrument)
WARD (hospital room with beds)   WARD (orphaned child)
WASTE (unused, physical decline, e.g., wasting disease)   WAIST (middle of body)
WEAK (feeble)   WEEK (seven days)
WEIGHT (heaviness, e.g., body weight)   WAIT (to remain, delay)
WEN (facial, warty growth)   WHEN (adverb of time)
YOLK (yellow part of egg)   YOKE (to join together)

American and British Spelling

Despite the widespread contact and transfer of expressions between Britain and America there are still some noticeable differences in spelling between the two countries.* Some of these variations are minor, such as the American ending -or for the British -our (e.g., color, colour) and -ter for -tre.

Groups of words in which spelling is different are as follows:

	American	British
or for *our*	color	colour
	endeavor	endeavour
	humor	humour
e for *oe*	celiac	coeliac
	diarrhea	diarrhoea
	edema	oedema
	esophagus	oesophagus
	estrogen	oestrogen
	fetus	foetus
e for *ae*	anemia	anaemia
	anesthetic	anaesthetic
	cecum	caecum
	defecation	defaecation
	etiology	aetiology
	hematuria	haematuria
	hemoglobin	haemoglobin
	pediatric	paediatric
ize or *ise*	analyze	analyse
Americans prefer -*ize* in	catheterize	catheterise
verbs and their derivatives.	cauterize	cauterise
British may use either.	criticize	criticise
	sensitize	sensitise
er for *re*	center	centre
	meter	metre
	saltpeter	saltpetre
	theater	theatre

* It must be pointed out that modern British usage increasingly reflects American spelling. The examples given here are, therefore, generalizations only.

	American	British
al omitted in ending when followed by *ic*	anatomic	anatomical
	histologic	histological
	physiologic	physiological
f for *ph*	sulfonamide	sulphonamide
	sulfur	sulphur
k for *c*	leukocyte	leucocyte
silent endings omitted	catalog	catalogue
	gram	gramme
	program	programme

Telephoning

The conversations presented below are taken from familiar situations in the field of medical practice as well as from more general situations when the telephone is used. The objective is to provide practice in fluent conversation. The Language Focus section concentrates on specific expressions typical of the preceding type of situation.

Fixing Appointments

Secretary: Dr. Wilson's office.

Dr. North: Oh, hello. This is Dan North from Pediatrics. I'd like a word with Dr. Wilson if it's possible.

Secretary: I'm sorry, but he left for Michigan this morning. He was, in fact, looking for you just before he left.

Dr. North: Oh. Well, could I make an appointment?

Secretary: Yes. I'll just look at his schedule. Er . . . how about July 20th at 11 a.m.?

Dr. North: That sounds fine. The 20th at 11 a.m. Thanks very much.

Secretary: Thank you. Goodbye.

Dr. North: Goodbye.

Dr. Howard: Hello, is that Psychiatry?

Dr. Dill: Yes, it is.

Dr. Howard: I'd like to speak to Dr. Dill, please.

Dr. Dill: This is Dr. Dill.

Dr. Howard: Hello, this is Bob Howard from St Joseph's. I wonder if I could have a quick word with you about a patient of mine. She's an anorectic. It's rather a similar case to the one I saw you about last January.

Dr. Dill: Okay. I'm afraid I can't talk just now. Would you like to come in and see me?

Dr. Howard: Yes, that'd be best.

Dr. Dill: Okay, let me get my appointment book. Does Friday morning suit you? Eleven thirty?

Dr. Howard: That's fine. Eleven thirty.

Dr. Dill: Okay, I'll see you then.
Dr. Howard: Right, bye.
Dr. Dill: Bye.

Language Focus

Could I make an appointment?
I'll just look at his schedule.
How about July 20th at 11 a.m.?
That sounds fine.
I wonder if I could have a quick word with you?
I'm afraid I can't talk just now.
Would you like to come in and see me?
Let me get my appointment book.
Does Friday suit you?
I'll see you then.

Changing Appointments

Dr. Bruce: Alan Bruce.
Dr. Hicks: It's Bernard Hicks here, Alan.
Dr. Bruce: Oh, hi, Bernard.
Dr. Hicks: About our meeting, Alan. I'm afraid I won't be able to make it. I'm tied up in A & E. I wonder if we could possibly move it to Wednesday?
Dr. Bruce: Er . . . Wednesday is not good for me. How about Thursday?
Dr. Hicks: Thursday's fine. Same time? 3 o'clock?
Dr. Bruce: Fine.
Dr. Hicks: Okay. See you then. Bye.
Dr. Bruce: Bye, Bernard.

Returning a Call

Dr. Chester: Hello, Dr. Wang?
Dr. Wang: Speaking.
Dr. Chester: Ah. Paul Chester here.
Dr. Wang: Oh. Hello, Dr. Chester.
Dr. Chester: You rang yesterday about that patient–the iron-overloaded one. I'm sorry I wasn't there to talk to you about it. Can I just run over it with you now?
Dr. Wang: Well, unfortunately I can't talk just now. Can I call you back in five minutes?
Dr. Chester: That'll be fine.
Dr. Wang : Talk to you in a few minutes.
Dr. Chester: Okay. Thank you. Bye.

Language Focus

About our meeting . . . .
I'm afraid I won't be able to make it.
I'm tied up.
I wonder if we could possibly move it to . . . .
Wednesday is not good for me.
Thursday's fine.
You rang yesterday about that patient.
I'm sorry I wasn't there.
Unfortunately I can't talk just now.
Can I call you back?
Talk to you in a few minutes.

Recorded Messages

Dr. Moody: This is Stella Moody speaking. I'm not in my office at the moment . . . . I expect to be back on the 22nd of January. Please leave your name, number, and message when you hear this signal. Thank you for calling.

Dr. Adrian: John Adrian here from Medical Exhibitions. I'm calling about the equipment you need for your display of the new X-ray machines at the Leeds Conference. We have a slight problem of space in the hall. Could you call me as soon as you get back? Thank you.

Sara Brieche: Hello, this is Sara Brieche speaking. I'm not at home at the moment but I'll be back tomorrow. Please leave your name, number, and message after the signal. Thank you.

Hideo Masuda: Hideo Masuda speaking. That's M-A-S-U-D-A. I was given your number by your secretary. I'm calling about your visit to Kyoto next month. Dr. Mori will meet you at the airport. That's Dr. Mori. I'll spell that: M-O-R-I. I'll call back the day after tomorrow. My home number is 03-687533.

Language Focus

I'm not in my office at the moment.
Please leave your name, number, and message after the signal.
John Adrian here.
I'm calling about . . . .
I'll be back tomorrow.
Could you call me as soon as you get back?
I'll spell that: M-O-R-I.

Getting Through

Switchboard: Edinburgh Royal Infirmary.
Dr. Patel: Hello, could I speak to the hospital administrator, please?

Switchboard: Who shall I say is calling?
Dr. Patel: It's Dr. Patel from Glasgow General.
Switchboard : One moment please . . . I'm sorry, the line's busy. Will you hold?
Dr. Patel: I'll hold.
Switchboard: I'm sorry, the secretary's line is still busy. Will you hold?
Dr. Patel: Er . . . I'll call back later. Thank you.
Switchboard: Thank you for calling.

Dr. Jones: Hello, is this Pathology?
Dr. Naylor: Yes, it is.
Dr. Jones: I'd like to speak to Professor Naylor, please.
Dr. Naylor: This is Dr. Naylor.
Dr. Jones: Hello, Professor Naylor. This is Alan Jones from Fellowes Laboratories. I'm calling about the rats we sent you earlier this week.
Dr. Naylor: Oh, you should speak to my colleague, Chris Grady. I'll put you through to her extension. Just in case you get cut off, her extension is 4592.
Dr. Jones: Thank you.

Language Focus

Could I speak to . . . ?
The line is busy.
Will you hold?
I'll put you through.
Who shall I say is calling?
I'll call back later.
I'm calling about . . . .
You should speak to . . . .
Just in case you get cut off, her extension is . . . .

Getting Information

Eric Holmes: Hello, Ron? Eric here.
Laboratory: Hello, Eric. What can I do for you?
Eric Holmes: I was wondering if you had the results.
Laboratory: Oh, yes, the results. We've got them.
Eric Holmes: Great.
Laboratory: Okay, here we go. Urea 2.6.
Eric Holmes: Urea 2.6.
Laboratory: Sodium 136.
Eric Holmes: 136.
Laboratory: Potassium 3.9.
Eric Holmes: 3.5.
Laboratory: No, that's 3.9.

Eric Holmes: Okay, 3.9.
Laboratory: And a total CO_2 of 23.
Eric Holmes: Total CO_2 of 23.
Laboratory: And that's it.
Eric Holmes: Er . . . do you have the salicylate level?
Laboratory: I'm afraid we don't have that yet. We'll get that to you this afternoon.
Eric Holmes: Great, thanks, Ron. I'll call you later.
Laboratory: Right. Talk to you later, Eric.
Eric Holmes: Okay, bye.

Dr. A: Hello, Akira, Bill here.
Dr. B: Hi Bill.
Dr. A: About this alcoholic cirrhotic.
Dr. B: Yes.
Dr. A: I meant to ask you this morning if you could just give me a brief clinical summary. You know, the family background and so on. I'd like to acquaint myself with . . . .
Dr. B: Right. I'll get that to you. I'll send it by mail.
Dr. A: Great. Thanks very much. That'd be very helpful.
Dr. B: Right. Okay.
Dr. A: Okay, bye.
Dr. B: Bye.

Language Focus

What can I do for you?
I was wondering if . . . .
Do you have . . . ?
I'm afraid we don't have . . . .
We'll get that to you . . . .
I'll call you later.
About this . . . .
I meant to ask you this morning if you could . . . .
I'll send it by mail.

Admitting a Patient (on the Telephone)

Dr. Minuchin: Hello.
Dr. Morita: Hello, this is Dr. Morita from Casualty. I have a 70-year-old man, Philip Benson, with a fractured right neck of femur.
Dr. Minuchin: Yes. Send him to Ward 3.
Dr. Morita: Okay.
Dr. Minuchin: Okay.
Dr. Morita: Thanks very much.

Dr. Minuchin: Bye.
Dr. Morita: Bye.

Switchboard: Queen Mary's Hospital.
Dr. Taylor: Er . . . waiting female surgeon, please.
Switchboard: I'll put you through.
Dr. Taylor: Hello?
Dr. Marks: Heloise Marks.
Dr. Taylor: Oh, hello. It's Tim Taylor from A & E at the Edinburgh Central.
Dr. Marks: Hello.
Dr. Taylor: Are you the surgeon?
Dr. Marks: That's right.
Dr. Taylor: I've got a young woman, a 30-year-old businesswoman referred up by her GP with a kind of pilonidal abscess for about 10 to 14 days.
Dr. Marks: Right.
Dr. Taylor: She's been on antibiotics, and, er, basically it needs to be incised.
Dr. Marks: Right.
Dr. Taylor: Can you take her?
Dr. Marks: Of course. What's the patient's name?
Dr. Taylor: Christabel Kilroy.
Dr. Marks: Okay. K-I-L-R-O-Y . . . Christabel. Good.
Dr. Taylor: I'll get her to pick up her nightclothes and . . . er . . . .
Dr. Marks: Okay. Lovely.
Dr. Taylor: . . . and she'll make her own way down.
Dr. Marks: Great.
Dr. Taylor: Okay. Thanks very much indeed.
Dr. Marks: You're welcome. Bye.

Language Focus

I have a 70-year-old man . . . with a . . . .
Send him to Ward 3.
I've got a young woman . . . referred up by her GP. . . .
She's been on antibiotics . . . .
. . . it needs to be incised.
Can you take her?
I'll get her to pick up her nightclothes . . . .
She'll make her own way down.

The Consultation

The consultation is a doctor-patient interview where a doctor tries to find out and treat a patient's problem. After the initial greetings, the doctor will usually ask what the patient has come for, what the symptoms are, how long the problem has been going on, and other questions about the patient's personal and social background. The doctor may then examine the patient. At the close of the consultation the doctor will normally give an assessment of the patient's problem, may prescribe medication, arrange for further tests, for referral to hospital, or some other course of action. The patient often asks questions at this point, before the close of the discussion.

Greetings and Identification

Good morning, Mrs. Davies. Do take a seat.
Come in and sit down, Mr. Wilson.
It's Mr. Alan, isn't it? Do take a seat.
Good morning, Mr. Chen. Have a seat.
I'm Dr. Graham.
Dr. Crane wrote to me about your little girl. Is it Jane?
My name's Dr. Simpson.
My name is Dr. Freeling, and I've read Dr. Wood's letter.

Present Complaint

Now, Mrs. Davies, what can I do for you?
Now, Mr. Wilson, what's troubling you?
Well, Mr. Alan, what's brought you here?
Well, Mr. Chen, what seems to be the problem?
Well, Mrs. Davies, I've read the letter from your doctor and he tells me you've been having headaches.
Now, Mr. Bogard, what's brought you along here today?

Taking a History

Questions to the patient may take various forms. We can categorize some types of questions as follows:

1. *What* questions
2. *How about* questions
3. *Where* questions
4. *When* questions
5. *How long* questions
6. *Do you ever* questions
7. *Do you suffer from* questions
8. *Have you ever* questions
9. *How much* questions
10. *How bad* questions

I. History of Present Illness

How long have you had this pain?
Where is the pain exactly?
Can you show me where it hurts?
When did you first notice this?
When did the trouble first start?
How long has this been going on?
How long have you had this problem?
Does the pain have any relation to . . . ?
Does it bother you when you are . . . ?
Do you ever feel like vomiting?

II. Taking a Past History

When asking questions about the patient's past, the form *Have you
ever* . . . ? is a common question form. Note that this form uses the present
perfect form of the verb.

Have you ever had chicken pox?
Did you ever have any fractures?
Have you ever been operated on?
Have you ever had your tonsils out?
How about your bowels? Have you ever had any problems?

III. Taking a Family History

When taking a family history, the present tense is often used, in particular
the forms *Do you have* . . . ? and *Is your* . . . ? *Are your* . . . ?

Are your parents alive? (Are your folks living?)
Do you have any brothers and sisters?
Can I ask you about your parents? Are they . . . ?
Are your parents in good health?
Are you married?
Do you have any children?
How about your relations with your husband?
Does your husband smoke (drink)?

What did your parents die of?
When did your wife die?

IV. Taking a Social History

Do your parents live with you?
How do you get on with your workmates?
How about your relations with your colleagues?
When did you move into town from the country?
How long have you lived in this country?
Do you socialize much?
Do you go out drinking much?

Review of the Systems

The nature of this review of the systems depends obviously on the type of illness presented, e.g., psychiatric, orthopedic, and so on. A review of the types of questions that the doctor asks the patient and some characteristic examination procedures are given on pages 89–96.

Doing a Physical Examination

The physical examination is carried out by means of a series of polite instructions to the patient. The verb forms most common in this situation are *Could you . . . ? Would you . . . ? Can you . . . ?* Note also the use of the adverbial expressions *just* and *for a second,* which tend to soften the strength of the instruction and reduce the potential embarrassment of the situation.

Okay. If you'd just like to slip off your pants?
Right. Could you just take off your skirt for a second?
Could you just hop onto the couch for a moment?
Would you lie flat on the couch for a moment?
Could you give me your arm?
Would you open your mouth wide?
Just hold out your arms for a second . . . Good.
Can you take a deep breath and hold it? Great.
Now blow the air out and hold it . . . Terrific.

(Treatment and) Closing the Consultation

Well, Mr. Chen, I can't see anything wrong here.
Well, Mr. Wilson, I don't think there's anything to worry about.
Okay, Mrs. Davies, I'm going to give you something to relieve the pain.
Okay, Mrs. Takahashi, we'll give you something to calm you down.
Right. We'll give you some tablets to ease the pain in your muscles, and then we'll get the physiotherapist to organize some exercises to strengthen those muscles.

Well, try these tablets for two weeks and see how you get on. Drop
in and see me again in about a month's time.
Well, I think we'll ask someone at the Central Hospital to have a look
at you. You should be hearing from them in about a week or so.
Right. I think we need to do a few tests . . . .
Well, Mrs. da Silva, we'll send these samples off to be tested, and
we'll let you know the results as soon as we get them.
Okay, Mrs. Hamid, I can't see anything seriously wrong here other
than some . . . . I'd like you to come back in two weeks, and we'll
see if you feel better. In the meantime, I'd like you to take these
tablets. I think they should help.

Taking a History: Review of the Systems

EXAMINING THE CHILD
Questioning the Parent

Does she sleep at the normal time?
Is he active, like other children?
Does she have a good appetite? Does she eat at the usual times?
When did his first tooth appear?
Does he pass wind as normal?
Is his toilet normal? Does he ever get diarrhea?
Does she have any rashes?
Does he ever bring up his food?
Has he ever had a fever?
Does she cough a lot?
Are you breastfeeding?
How often do you feed him?
Do you give him liquids?

Examination Procedure

Suspend the baby by its chest.
Plot the measurement of its head. See if the neck is rigid.
Abduct the thigh.
Stimulate the baby's palm.
Flex the knee and hip.
Take the pulse (temperature, blood pressure).
Listen to the chest.
Look for any rash on the body.
Palpate the abdomen.
Check the baby's weight and height.

OTORHINOLARYNGOLOGY EXAMINATION
Questioning the Patient

Do you ever have nose bleeds?
Is there any bad smell from your nose?

Does your nose run a lot?
How long has your voice been hoarse?
Do you have a sore throat?
Do you have bad breath?
Do you often have a fever?
Do you feel any pain inside your ears?
Which one is worse?
Is there any discharge from your ears?
Are you having any difficulty with your hearing?
Does it hurt when you swallow?

Examination Procedure

Have the patient look down/straight ahead.
Inspect the base of the tongue.
Hold the tip of the tongue.
Steady the tongue.
Insert a speculum.
Check the throat for any growth (congestion).
Inspect the ear for any discharge.
Test the patient's hearing.
Whisper in the ear.
Inspect the tonsils.

RESPIRATORY EXAMINATION
Questioning the Patient

Do you cough a lot?
Do you ever get short of breath?
What brings on your cough?
Do you ever bring something up? Is it thick or light?
What color is the stuff you bring up?
Do you have any chest pains after exercise?
Any pains in your chest when you cough?
Do you wheeze?
How is your appetite?
Do you sweat at night?
Do you cough when you smell certain foods or other smells?
Do you ever get short of breath?
Do you smoke?
What is your job?

Examination Procedure

Smell the patient's breath.
Observe his chest during breathing.
Palpate (percuss) the chest. Auscultate the chest.

Measure the chest on inspiration and expiration.
Inspect the throat with a laryngoscope.
Check the nails for clubbing.
Take an X-ray.

CARDIOVASCULAR EXAMINATION
Questioning the Patient

Do your legs swell?
Do you get tired easily?
Do you get out of breath easily?
Do you have palpitations?
Is there any heart disease in the family?
Do you get any pains in the chest?
Do you cough much?
What brings on your cough?
Do you ever feel giddy?
How about sore throats?
Do you get headaches?
Are you nervous or anxious about anything?

Examination Procedure

Take the patient's blood pressure.
Apply the cuff.
Inflate the cuff.
Deflate the cuff.
Record the systolic/diastolic pressure.
Identify the heart sound.
Feel for the vibration of the thrill.
Time the thrill.
Palpate the impulse.

OBSTETRICAL AND GYNECOLOGICAL EXAMINATION
Questioning the Patient

When was your last period? Was it heavy? Was it painful?
  How long did it last?
When did your periods start?
Are your periods regular?
How many children have you had? How old is your last child?
Have you had any miscarriages?
Do you have any vaginal discharge?
How long have you had this discharge?
What's the color of this discharge?
Does it have a bad smell?
Do you feel any pain while passing urine?

Is sexual intercourse painful?
Do you feel any vaginal pain or discomfort?

Examination Procedure

Feel for masses in the breast (or a palpable lesion in the lower abdomen),
    outline it,
    move it,
    knead it,
    ballot it,
    percuss it.
Take a pap smear.
Do a tomography.
Take a biopsy.
Do a PV examination.
Take an X-ray.
Measure the circumference of the abdomen.
Check the position of the fetus.

OPTHALMOLOGICAL EXAMINATION
Questioning the Patient

Do your eyes get tired easily?
Do your eyes get red easily?
Do you ever see double (distorted) images in front of your eyes?
Do you ever see unusual shapes before your eyes?
Do you have headaches?
Do you get headaches when you're reading?
Do your eyes itch?
Do your eyes water?
Do they water when you read?
Do you find that you're losing your eyelashes?
Are you short-sighted?
Are you long-sighted? How long have you had this problem with your vision?
Do you have any discharge from your eyes?
Do the lashes come away in this discharge, especially in the morning?
Do your eyeballs feel painful?
Have you had any diseases in the family . . . like diabetes or high blood pressure?

Examination Procedure

Give an eye test.
Observe the light reflex in the eye.

Observe the color of the rim.
Check the eye movements for diplopia and protrusion.
Observe the optic disc and vessels in the fundus.
Do a fundoscopy.
Check for visual acuity.
Check the eyeball movements to determine the activity of
    different muscles.
Note any discharge or watering of the eyes.

NEUROLOGICAL EXAMINATION
Questioning the Patient

Do you get headaches?
Do you know when these headaches are coming on?
Do you feel sick when you get these headaches?
Do you ever have dizzy spells?
Have you ever fainted?
Have you ever blacked out?
Do you see spots in front of your eyes?
Have you ever had a head injury?
Do you feel agitated? Never, or some of the time?
Are you a heavy drinker?

Examination Procedure

Test motor and sensory systems.
Elevate the mandible.
Deviate the mandible.
Determine the visual acuity of each eye.
Observe the fundi.
Test abdominal reflexes for sensitivity.
Flex the legs.
Determine the rigidity and flexibility of various muscles.

GENITO-URINARY EXAMINATION
Questioning the Patient

Do you drink a lot?
Have you noticed any blood in your urine?
Does it burn when you urinate?
Do you strain when you urinate?
Do you ever wet the bed?
How many times do you have to go during the night?
Do you often get diarrhea, constipation?
Do your bowel movements smell bad?

I'd like a sample of your urine.
Does your urine dribble?

Examination Procedures (Male)

Examine the prostate.
Palpate the kidneys.
Check for any swelling of the scrotum.
Examine the testes.

MUSCULOSKELETAL EXAMINATION
Questioning the Patient

Does it hurt if you bend your knee?
Do you have any difficulty moving your arms or legs?
Have you had any falls?
Do you feel any weakness in your limbs?
Can you tell me exactly how you turned your foot?
Can you bend over and touch your toes?
Can I just have you walk to the door and back?
Does the knee feel tender here?
Do your muscles feel stiff in the morning?
Have you noticed any twitching of your muscles?

Examination Procedure

Palpate the heel for swelling (synovial thickening/bursitis).
Check the heel for rupture.
Rotate the forefoot.
Extend the knee.
Flex the knee.
Palpate the ribs.
Check the patient's reflexes.
Take a blood test.
Do an X-ray.

PSYCHIATRIC INTERVIEW
Questioning the Patient

How do you get on with other people?
Do you find you can trust people?
Do you sometimes feel picked upon?
Do you think people like you generally?
Are you self-conscious?
Do you ever find that your thoughts stop dead and leave your
    mind a complete blank?

Do you ever feel completely possessed by another person?
Do you ever feel controlled from outside like a puppet or robot?
Is your mood stable, or does it change greatly from day to day?
Would you describe yourself as a happy and contented person?
Do people think of you as a happy-go-lucky person, the life-and-soul of the party, or perhaps rather gloomy and unhappy?
Do you have many friends?
Would you describe yourself as shy?
Do you ever get into a furious rage?
Have you ever hurt anyone?
Do you often lose your temper?
Do you always follow a set routine?
Do you prefer things to be neat and tidy?
Do you ever tend to check things more than once or twice?
Are you sometimes overly emotional?
Do you like to be the center of attention?
Do you tend to rely on other people a great deal?
Have you usually got lots of energy?
Do you find it difficult to cope with the demands of everyday life?
Have you ever been in trouble with the police?
Do you dislike being told what to do?
Do you sometimes feel like hurting people?

DENTAL EXAMINATION
Questioning the Patient

Can you tell me which tooth is causing the problem?
Where is it sore – the top teeth or bottom teeth?
Is it sore all the time?
What sorts of things make it sore?
Is it hot things? Cold things? Sweet things?
Is it a localized or a general pain?
Is it sore to touch?
Would it be sore if I were to tap the tooth?
How long have your gums been bleeding?
Have you had an anesthetic before?
Are you taking any medicines at the moment?
When was the last time you visited your dentist?

Examination Procedure

Excavate a cavity.
Ream a root.
Extract a tooth.
Scrape the surface.
Clean out the filling.
Prepare a tooth for crowning.
Cement a crown.
Mix the amalgam.
Pack an amalgam.
Place a lining in the cavity.
Fill the tooth.
Smooth the surface.
Polish the surface.

Doctor-Patient Conversations

In the following section a number of conversations between doctors and patients are presented. They illustrate many of the language points raised in the previous sections about greetings and identification, taking a history, closing, etc. Because these conversations are taken from both American and British situations a few words are needed on the different grades of medical staff in hospitals in the USA and in Britain.

Notes on Medical Staff in the USA and in Britain

The general equivalents of positions in the two systems (the British N.H.S [National Health Service] and the USA) can be schematized as follows:

USA	Britain
Attending Physician	Consultant
Senior Resident (Chief Resident)	Senior Registrar
3rd/2nd Year Resident	Registrar
1st Year Resident	Senior House Officer
Intern	House Officer

Interns (US) and House Officers (Britain) are recent graduates of a medical or dental school who receive supervised practical training in a hospital by assisting in the medical and surgical care of patients. Residents (US) and Registrars (Britain) are doctors seeking to qualify as specialists in a field of medicine or dentistry. In the US they are termed "resident surgeon" or "resident pediatrician" as the case may be. In Britain, a Senior Registrar can hold a post for four years; in the US a Senior Resident holds this post for one year only. Consultants (Britain) and Attending Physicians (US) are the most senior grades in a hospital. The team of doctors and assistants under the Consultant are known as a "firm."A House Officer might say, for example: "I'm in Mr. Kendall's firm." Surgeons are addressed as "Mr." (Mister) in Britain, and other specialists as "Doctor."

A "GP" (General Practitioner) is a "family doctor" who is not based in hospital but has a medical practice within the local community and is closely identified with it. The family doctor system is considered to be an important feature of the British National Health Service. Patients requiring further attention by specialists, or certain tests, may be referred by a local GP to a nearby hospital.

THE SHOPKEEPER (HEADACHES)

GP: Good morning, I'm Dr. Garcia.

Patient: Good morning, doctor

GP: It's Ms. Coleman, isn't it?

Patient: That's right. I saw you about six months ago with a broken finger.

GP: Yes, of course. And is that all healed now?

Patient: It's fine. No problems.

GP: Okay. What can I do for you today?

Patient: Well, I've been having these headaches. They started about two months ago. They seem to come on quite suddenly, and I get dizzy spells as well.

GP: Right. Let's start with the headaches. Er . . . when . . . how would you describe them?

Patient: Well, it's a kind of dull . . . it's difficult to describe actually . . . a kind of tension . . . a sort of tightness . . . compression.

GP: Where is the pain exactly? Can you show me?

Patient: It's frontal. In the front here. I thought it might be my eyes.

GP: Do you wear glasses?

Patient: No, I don't.

GP: You used the word *tension*. What made you use that word?

Patient: Well, it's just the feeling I get; the headaches, I mean.

GP: How long do these headaches last?

Patient: Sometimes ten minutes; sometimes an hour.

GP: And how often are you getting them?

Patient: Er . . . once a day, twice a day.

GP: Now, do these headaches come on at any particular time?

Patient: Yeah, when I go to work in the morning. When I step outside. My shop . . . I run a boutique . . . my shop's just nearby, so when I walk out the headache comes on.

GP: Do you ever get these headaches at night?

Patient: No, but I'm not sleeping at night. I wake up two or three times every night.

GP: Why is that?

Patient: Well, I think I'm a bit of a worrier. We've had staff problems at work, and . . . the financial situation's very precarious at the moment. I really don't know how things'll turn out.

GP: Well, I'm sorry to hear about that. Can I just come back for a moment to these "dizzy spells"? Can you describe them?

Patient: Well, they last a few seconds. I suddenly feel really dizzy. I was very bad on one occasion. I was staggering about for . . . it must have been about half a minute. I broke out into a sweat. It was really worrying, actually. Maybe I'm just overdoing it. I'm doing a lot of overtime now, and I'm not really getting enough rest, I know.

GP: This dizziness . . . To some people it's a sensation of falling – to other people it's a sensation of fainting. Do you see the distinction I'm . . . Do you see what I'm getting at? How would you describe your dizziness?

Patient: Well, I feel as if I'm going to fall down.

GP: Have you ever had the sensation when you're not standing up?

Patient: Well, coming back from work once. I was in my car.

GP: About your health in general. How do you feel in general?

Patient: No problems. The odd cold. But that's about it.

GP: Okay. Let me give you a check-over. We'll start with your eyesight . . . Could you just look this way . . . ? Look at the light . . . Are you going to have your eyes tested?

Patient: Yes, I have an appointment next week.

GP: Have you noticed any problems with your eyesight?

Patient: Well, my boyfriend says I'm always screwing up my eyes when I'm watching the television. He says when I'm reading the paper I squint.

GP: Have you got a cough or a spit?

Patient: No.

GP: Any breathlessness?

Patient: No.

GP: No pains in the chest?

Patient: No.

GP: Do you have any trouble urinating?

Patient: No.

GP: Your periods regular?

Patient: Uh-huh.

GP: Can I turn to your family? Your parents? Are they . . . ?

Patient: They're fine. My two sisters live with them. I have an apartment in the center of town.

GP: Okay. Let me check you over . . .

(PHYSICAL EXAMINATION)

GP: Well, I've checked you over pretty thoroughly and I can't find anything wrong. It sounds to me as if you've been overdoing things.

Patient: I have.

GP: Exactly how much extra work are you doing now? I mean, you mentioned overtime. Do you take time off at the weekends?

Patient: Well, I've had to work Saturdays and Sundays. On Sundays I do the accounts. Our accountant left suddenly but we're getting a new man next week.

GP: Well, I think these headaches could be connected to the fact that you're under a great deal of strain. I think you've got to make more time for yourself – more time to relax. Now I can give you something to relax you a little, but I think we might wait a bit. What's your opinion?

Patient: I'd rather not be on tranquilizers if I can help it. I'm relieved that nothing's actually wrong.

GP: I really can't see anything wrong; you seem to be in good health.

Patient: Well, as you say, I need to calm down a bit.

GP: Take Sunday off – completely. Go out for the day. You mentioned the new accountant. When does he start?

Patient: Next week. It should make a lot of difference.

GP: Okay, I want you to take things easier. See if you can share your responsibilities more, so that you get more time to relax. And go and get your eyes seen to. That's next week, is it?

Patient: Next week.

GP: Great. Okay. Now, I'd like you to come in and see me in a couple of weeks. Tell me how things are getting on.

Patient: Good. Thanks very much, doctor.

GP: Okay. We'll see you again. Bye.

Patient: Goodbye. Thanks very much.

THE LAWYER (GASTRIC ULCER) – SECOND VISIT

Resident: Good morning, Mr. Thompson. Good to see you again.

Patient: Morning, doctor.

Resident: You were here in . . . er . . . . It was March, wasn't it?

Patient: Right.

Resident: And we found you had an ulcer.

Patient: Yeah; gave me quite a shock.

Resident: And how are you feeling?

Patient: Just fine.

Resident: Okay. Good. You're not vomiting now?

Patient: No, no. It was bad before. I was throwing up all the time, but not now.

Resident: And you've cut out the drinking?

Patient: Yes, I have. Haven't touched the stuff since . . . er . . . .

Resident: Do you have any trouble with your bowels?

Patient: No.

Resident: No black-looking stool?

Patient: No.

Resident: Good. And what medication are you taking now?

Patient: The Alinex K. I'm taking one in the morning.

Resident: And what else are you taking?

Patient: That's all.

Resident: You've stopped the ones at night.

Patient: Yeah. I stopped them a couple of weeks ago.

Resident. And you've had no trouble with indigestion since you stopped those?

Patient: No.

Resident: And do you ever take aspirins or anything like that?

Patient: Well, very occasionally I take a couple of Tylenol.

Resident: Uh-huh.

Patient: You know – when I have a headache or something.

Resident: Uh-huh. You're not taking any of your Pepto-Bismol any more.

Patient: No.

Resident: I think I should listen to your chest again. Check out your heart again.

Patient: Right.

Resident: And we also want to check the blood . . . see if that's gotten any better.

Patient: Okay.

Resident: Would you like to step through into the next room and remove your shirt? Would you just like to lie down on the couch? I'll just feel your stomach here . . . Okay, fine. Now, I just want to take your blood pressure as well. Okay? If you'd just raise your arm a little . . . Fine . . . Good . . . I'll just take a blood sample as well. Just keep your arm straight there. Fine. There'll be a little prick—like a mosquito bite. Okay, there we go. Okay. I'll send that sample off and we'll check it. If the sample is okay we won't need to go on seeing you any more.

Patient: So you think I'm getting better.

Resident: Absolutely. I think it's all settling down now. I'll just put this Band-aid on your arm and . . . er . . . you can take it off when you get home.

Patient: Thanks a lot.

Resident: You can put your shirt on, and when you're ready go straight through to reception. The nurse'll check your card.

Patient: Well, thanks very much, doctor . . . I appreciate it.

Resident: You're welcome.

Patient: Thanks a lot. Goodbye.

Resident: Goodbye.

THE FIREFIGHTER (PALPITATIONS)

GP: Good morning, Mr. Lane. I'm Dr. Wong.

Patient: Morning, doctor.

GP: Now, what can I do for you?

Patient: Well, doctor, it's these . . . it's like cramp across my chest. Not cramp, really, but it feels as if it's going to be cramp. Do you know what I mean?

GP: And how long has this been going on?

Patient: About a month. Well, I guess it's about seven weeks now . . .

GP: Tell me . . .

Patient: . . . but I haven't had anything yesterday or today.

GP: Yes. When you say it's "like cramp". . .

Patient: Well, if I've been lying in bed for instance, it might come on, and then it goes away before it goes into cramp.

GP: How long does it last?

Patient: Oh, a few seconds.

GP: You said it's not painful. Can you describe it?

Patient: Well, it's a kind of fluttering. Like a nerve.

GP: And have you been getting it every day or . . .

Patient: Yes, every day.

GP: Only at work?

Patient: No, I was getting it in the house as well.

GP: Was there anything that might bring it on?

Patient: Well, when I'm at work, I could be operating one of the machines . . . you know, the machines we use for fire drills . . . operating the ladders . . . and it'd come on then, more than other times.

GP: Was there any other position that might bring it on?

Patient: Well, I've been sitting in the house and it's happened.

GP: How about walking?

Patient: I've had a fluttering when I'm out walking, but it's more often when I'm at the machine.

GP: Do you relate it in any way to meals?

Patient: No.

GP: You don't think it's likely to come on before or after meals?

Patient: No.

GP: How many episodes a day were you getting?

Patient: About . . . I guess . . . one or two a day.

GP: And on the worst day you ever had, how many times did you have it then?

Patient: Oh, I must have had it every hour.

GP: And the longest episode lasted for?

Patient: Seconds.

GP: And when you had it were you in any other way upset? Were you breathless?

Patient: Well, at work . . . I'm doing very technical work . . . I do worry about my job. I have to get things right. If I make a mistake . . . you know . . . So I do worry about my job.

GP: Were you breathless with this discomfort?

Patient: No.

GP: Did you think something terrible was going to happen?
Patient: Well, I got a fright at first, but then it just went away. And then it came back again. I just sort of got used to it.
GP: Were you aware of palpitations? Do you know what I mean by palpitations?
Patient: That's a quickening of the heart rate.
GP: Yes.
Patient: No, no.
GP: How's your health otherwise?
Patient: Fine.
GP: Okay. Do you mind if I check up on you?

(PHYSICAL EXAMINATION)

GP: Do you have any cough or phlegm?
Patient: No.
GP: Do your ankles ever swell up?
Patient: No, but I go over very easily on my ankles.
GP: How about urinating?
Patient: No. Well, I'm up every night.
GP: How many times?
Patient: Once. Once every night.
GP: And what's the stream like?
Patient: All right.
GP: Putting it bluntly, could you hit that bucket from where you're standing?
Patient: Easy.
GP: Have you ever noticed any blood in the urine?
Patient: No.
GP: How about your weight; is it steady?
Patient: Yes.
GP: Indigestion?
Patient: None at all.
GP: And your bowels? Have they changed?
Patient: They're all right.
GP: Now is your eyesight all right?
Patient: No problem.
GP: No headaches?
Patient: Well, I get the odd headache – not severe.
GP: Where are these headaches?
Patient: Just above my eyes, you know. Just a dull ache.
GP: Alcohol?
Patient: I drink at weekends . . . a couple of beers and a few rums.
GP: Do you smoke?

Patient: No.

GP: Who's in the house with you?

Patient: My wife.

GP: Just the two of you? Children?

Patient: No.

GP: Any brothers and sisters?

Patient: Yes.

GP: How many do you have?

Patient: Two brothers and one sister.

GP: Are they fit and well?

Patient: Uh-huh.

GP: There's nobody with blood pressure trouble in the family?

Patient: No.

GP: Or kidney trouble in the family?

Patient: No.

GP: Is there anybody with heart trouble?

Patient: My mother died when she was 56 with heart trouble. That was 20 years ago.

GP: Anybody else? Nobody else in the family?

Patient: No. I think we're all fit, really. Well, I've been wondering whether, you know, whether there's something wrong with my heart.

GP: Well, I've examined you, and I can be very reassuring. I can't find anything at all. But if you come to me – if anybody of your age comes to me and says they've got a pain in the chest, the first thing I have to do is to be quite certain this is not a heart pain, although taking a history from you there's nothing to suggest that this is a heart problem. But what I'm going to do is send you to the University Hospital for some tests . . . a cardiogram, X-ray, and also to have your blood looked at.

You know, we often get people coming along with, you know, unusual aches and pains . . . and then they settle down, and we never know what it was.

Patient: Well, I just wanted to be sure.

GP: Absolutely. You did the right thing to come. We'll send you along to the hospital and have these tests done. Okay?

Patient: Right.

GP: I wish you all the best in the meantime.

Patient: Okay. Thanks very much.

GP: If you go outside, the nurse at reception will see to you. Bye for now.

Patient: Bye.

THE WARD ROUND (POSTOPERATIVE)

Consultant: Good morning, Mr. Walton.

Patient: Good morning.

Consultant: You've met my colleague, Mr. Sekiya.

Resident: How do you do.

Patient: Hello.

Consultant: So, did you have a comfortable night?

Patient: No, not really.

Consultant: Sorry to hear that. And how are you feeling at the moment?

Patient: A bit better.

Consultant: You don't feel sick at all?

Patient: No, I'm okay.

Consultant: That's good. Are you having sips of water?

Patient: No.

Consultant: Would you like some?

Patient: Well, I don't really feel like . . .

Consultant: Ah. You can't drink anything at the moment.

Patient: The nurses have been giving me mouthwashes.

Consultant: Yes. I think you'll begin to pick up as the day goes on. And
. . . er . . . we'll carry on giving you something to ease the discomfort.
Does it hurt much?

Patient: Well, it does when I move about.

Consultant: Right. But the sooner we have you on the move the quicker
you'll start to heal. So, we'll have you sitting in the chair this afternoon,
enjoying the sunshine.

Patient: Okay. I can't say I'm really looking forward to that.

Consultant: Mm. You had a pretty big gallstone. And the gallbladder was
quite inflamed. There was a lot of infection around it and inside it. Well,
it's out now, so no need to worry about it. It won't cause you any more
trouble.

Patient: Mm.

Consultant: Now, you've got a little drain coming out the side –

Patient: Yes.

Consultant: – that'll come out in a few days' time.

Patient: Great.

Consultant: Any questions, or anything we can do for you?

Patient: No, I think I'm okay. I'm feeling a bit woozy at the moment. Oh,
when will my wife be able to come and see me? The nurses told me
before, but I can't remember.

Consultant: Dr. Sekiya, I think you're the person to answer that one.

Resident: Yes, the visiting hours are from 6 to 8 this evening.

Patient: Okay, thank you. She'll be here tonight in that case.

Consultant: Fine. Well, we'll stop in to see you tomorrow.

Patient: Thank you.

Consultant: Okay. See you tomorrow.

Patient: Thank you.

Consultant: Bye.
Patient: Bye.
Resident: Goodbye.
Patient: Goodbye.

Understanding Symptoms

EXPRESSIONS USED BY PATIENTS

These are some expressions people use in conversation with one another or with a doctor. They describe how a person feels, or they identify specific health problems.

Notice the contracted forms *I've* and *I'm*. They are very common in spoken English. Note also that *I've got . . .*, indicating possession, is more common in British English than in American English, where *I have . . .* is the usual form. Both forms are used freely in the expressions below. Words followed by the letter (*v.*), denoting "vulgar," are not used in polite conversation.

Scalp and Hair

I've got dandruff.
My scalp's flaky (lumpy/bumpy).
My scalp itches (my scalp's itchy).
My hair's infested with lice.
I'm suffering from (I have . . .) nits (lice/vermin/insects).
My hair's greasy (dry/brittle/receding).
My hair's falling out (dropping out/coming out).
I'm going bald (losing my hair).
I'm getting a bald patch.
I've got split ends.

Head

I've got a headache.
I've got a splitting (dreadful/awful/terrible/bad) headache.
My head aches (throbs).
My head's aching.
I've got a bad head.
I've got a migraine.
I come over (I feel) woozy (funny/queer/light-headed/peculiar)
    when I get up suddenly.
I feel woozy (faint/dizzy).

107

I feel drowsy.
I feel giddy.
I feel the room spinning.
The room's spinning.
The room spins when . . . .
Everything goes round.
I see stars when . . . .
I've split my head (scalp/skull) open.
I had a blackout.
I blacked out (fainted).

Eyes

I can't see out my left (right) eye.
My eyes hurt (ache/sting/itch).
My eyes are sore (bloodshot).
I've got eyestrain.
I've got a pain in my left (right) eye.
Everything's fuzzy (blurred) round the edges.
I'm seeing spots (in front of my eyes).
I'm short-sighted.
I'm blind as a bat.
My vision's blurred.
I'm long-sighted (far-sighted).
My eyes are red (pink/cloudy/milky).
I'm blue round the eyes.
My eyes are itchy (I've got itchy eyes).
My eyes are watering a lot.
I'm seeing double (I see double) when I . . . .
I've got something in my eye.
I've got red eye.
I've got a stye.

Ears

My ear aches (I've got earache).
I've got ringing (buzzing/humming/banging) in my ears.
My ears feel (are) bunged up (clogged/blocked up).
I think I'm going deaf.
I can't hear as well as I used to.
My ear's discharging (running).
I have waxy ears (wax in my ears).

Nose

My nose is blocked (bunged up/congested/red/sore/itchy/snotty/
   swollen).

I've got catarrh.
I've got a nosebleed.
I keep getting (having) nosebleeds.
My nose keeps running (I've got a runny nose).
I keep sneezing.
My sinuses are blocked.

Mouth

(a) Teeth
My tooth aches (throbs).
My gums are swollen (I've got swollen gums).
My gums are receding (I've got receding gums).
My wisdom tooth's erupting (impacted/in agony/giving me trouble).
I have an abscess.
My gums are bleeding.
I've got mouth ulcers.
I have buck teeth.

(b) Tongue
My tongue's black (furry/white/coated/yellow).
My mouth (tongue) feels (is) dry (numb/furry).
I have bad breath.

(c) Lips
My lips are (feel) swollen (sore/cracked/dry/chapped/flaky/numb/ bruised).
I've (got/keep getting) cold sores (a cut lip/a split lip).

Throat

I've got a sore throat (my throat's sore).
I have a bad throat.
My throat aches.
I'm hoarse (croaky).
I've got (I keep getting) a frog in my throat.
I've lost my voice.
My voice is hoarse.
I feel a tightness in my throat.
I can't breathe.
I can't swallow.
Food seems to stick in my throat.

Neck

I've got a stiff neck.
My glands are swollen (I've got swollen glands).
I have a crick in my neck.
I've cricked (ricked) my neck.

My neck aches.
I strained my neck.

Shoulders

I've got stiff shoulders.
I've twisted (yanked/pulled/wrenched/strained) (a muscle in) my
    shoulder.
My shoulders ache.
My shoulders are stiff (sore/painful/throbbing).
I've bruised my shoulder.

Back

My back aches (throbs).
I have backache.
I've pulled (wrenched/twisted) a muscle in my back.
I've done my back in.
I've wrenched (strained/ricked) my back.
I've got a bad back.
My back's bad.
I think I've slipped a disc.
I have sciatica (rheumatism/fibrosis/lumbago).

Arms/Hands

I've twisted (strained) my wrist.
I've strained my elbow.
I've got a pain in my elbow.
My hands feel cold.
I've got frostbite.
I feel a tingling sensation in my fingers.
I have chilblains.
My fingers are (have gone) numb.
My hands are sweaty (hot/cold/warty).
My palms are sweaty (I've got sweaty palms).
My fingers tremble a lot.
My hands have started shaking.
I've got B.O. (B.O. = body odor).
I smell under the armpits.
I've got warts on my hands (fingers).
I have white patches (spots) on my nails.
My nails break off easily (keep breaking/chip easily).

Chest

I feel a tightness in my chest.
I've got a pain under my ribs.

I get out of breath easily.
I find it difficult to breathe.
I'm fighting (gasping) for breath.
My tubes are all bunged up.
My lungs are clogged up.
I'm bringing up (coughing up) phlegm (blood/mucus).
I'm bringing up (coughing up) green (greeny yellow/yellow/brown/
   red/bloody/frothy) stuff.
My chest's bad (I've got a bad chest).
I'm coughing my guts up.
I've got a bad (terrible/hacking/racking) cough.
My heart keeps missing (skipping/jumping) a beat.
I've got a wheezy chest.
My breasts hurt (ache/are tender/are swollen).
I've got a discharge from my nipple(s).
I have a lump in my breast (under my arm).

Stomach

I've got stomach ache (tummy-ache/stomach upset/cramps in my
   stomach).
I have an upset tummy.
I've got a gippy tummy (bad stomach).
My stomach is funny.
I can't keep anything down.
I've got indigestion (heartburn/wind).
I get nauseated (I feel sick).
I feel like I'm going to vomit (spew/puke/throw up/be sick/barf).
I keep retching (barfing).
I can't bear to look at food.
I've got a gassy stomach.
I've got a poor appetite.
I don't have any appetite.
I'm (I've gone) off my food.

Bowels and Bladder

I've got diarrhea.
I'm incontinent.
I keep wetting myself.
I keep having (have) the occasional accident.
I sometimes leak.
I've got a weak bladder.
I've got the runs (trots/shits [v.]).
I keep farting (v.).
I've got a lot of wind.

I've got constipation (I'm constipated).
I can't go (to the toilet/loo/bog).
I can't take a shit (v.).
I can't pass water (pee [v.]/piss[v.]/wee).
My stool (shit[v.]/crap[v.]/excreta/motions) is runny (hard/watery/
    like bullets/well formed/loose).
My urine is yellowish (reddish/straw-colored).
I get a burning sensation when urinating.
I've noticed blood in my urine.
I've got piles.

Genital Organs

I have pain in my testicles (penis).
I can't get it up.
I can't get an erection.
I can't keep it up.
I can't climax (get an orgasm/come).
I strained my groin.
I had a hernia.
I'm impotent (frigid).
I come too early.
I've got a problem with premature ejaculation.
I feel pain when having sex.
I've been having a discharge from my vagina.
I've got a vaginal discharge.
I have trouble down below (down there/downstairs/with the
    plumbing).
I've missed a period.
I'm late (overdue).
I'm pregnant (expecting/going to have a baby).

Legs

I've pulled a muscle in my leg.
I've pulled a hamstring muscle.
I get a cramp in my leg (calves/thigh).
I've torn a ligament.
I've snapped a tendon in my leg (thigh).
I can't bend my legs.
My knee hurts.
My knees are stiff.
I've got a cartilage problem.
I have water on the knee.
I get pain in my shins.
I get a pain in the back of my legs.

I've bruised my leg.
My foot keeps going to sleep.
I get pins and needles in my legs (feet).
I've got chilblains in my toes.
I've got cramp in my thigh.
I have varicose veins.

Feet

I've sprained (twisted/turned) my ankle.
I went over on my ankle.
My ankle gave.
I've got a pain in my heel.
I have a burning sensation in the soles of my feet.
I've got blisters.
I've got an ingrown toenail.
I get cramp in my toes.
I have chilblains.
My ankles are swollen (have been swelling).
I've got swelling of the ankles.
I've got a verruca (athletes foot).

Skin

I've got a rash (come out in a rash/broken out in a rash).
My skin's blotchy (greasy/flaky/dry/clammy).
I feel itchy.
I've got sensitive skin.
I keep scratching.
My skin's peeling (flaking/weeping).
My skin's turned yellow.
I've got blackheads (whiteheads/open pores/spots/acne/pimples).
I have an acne problem.
I am badly sunburned.
I've got a mole that's getting bigger in size.

Mental State

I'm (I feel) depressed (fed up/listless/tired/exhausted/bored/moody/
miserable/down in the dumps/weepy/upset/afraid/frightened/
terrified/unhappy/confused/nervy/irritable/bad-tempered/edgy/
under the weather/aggravated/pissed off/like I'm knocking my
head on a brick wall/bogged down/at the end of my tether/out
of sorts).
I want to commit suicide (do away with myself/do myself in).
I'm afraid of doing myself an injury.
I can't cope.

I can't go on.
I've had enough.
I always have an uneasy feeling.
Everything seems to irritate me (I get easily irritated).
I feel hateful about everything.
I've become very short-tempered.
I'm in no mood to do anything.
I'm afraid to go out.
I don't feel myself.
I'm always brooding.
My memory's going.
Nothing seems worth bothering about any more.
I have difficulty in remembering things.
I've no confidence in myself.
I've been hearing voices.
I've been timid (introverted) since I was a child.
I'm always on edge.
I worry about little things.
My nerves are bad.
I feel hopeless.
I'm in a constant state of anxiety.

Sleep

I can't get to sleep.
I suffer from insomnia.
I can't wake up in the mornings.
All I want to do is sleep.
I have nightmares (bad dreams).
I snore.
I talk (walk) in my sleep.

The Language of Doctor and Patient

The people who provide medical care and who possess specialized knowledge, such as doctors and nurses, often use a specialized vocabulary, especially when communicating between themselves. This "language" is not always shared by their "customers" – the patients – who have their own expressions for describing illnesses, symptoms, parts of the body, and so on. A selection of common medical terms and their general, everyday equivalents are given below.

1. Note that, despite what has been said above, many "medical" terms are commonly understood and used by many patients.

2. Some words are followed by the letter (v.). These are expressions not used in polite conversation, but rather when a speaker wishes to be obscene, vulgar, or offensive. They are likely to cause embarrassment or anger if used in the wrong situations.

Medical Description	*General Description*
Brain	
cranium	skull
cerebral palsy	Little's disease
cerebral concussion	concussion, to be knocked out
convulsion	fit
delirium tremens	the DTs, the shakes
epilepsy	fits, to have fits
encephalitis lethergica	sleepy sickness/sleeping sickness
encephalitis	brain fever
thrombosis, embolism, cerebral hemorrhage	apoplexy, stroke, blood clot
transient ischemic episode	small stroke
neuralgia	face ache (can be in other places, e.g., back)
conjunctivitis	pink eye
exophthalmos	bulging eyes, protruding eyes
hordeolum	stye
myopia (myopic)	short-sight, to be short-sighted
orbis	eye socket
retinitis	inflammation, redness of the retina
strabismus	squinting, to squint
Rhodopsin	visual purple

Medical Description	*General Description*
Ear, Nose, and Throat	
coryza	cold in the head, head cold
thyroid cartilage (of the larynx)	Adam's apple
epidemic parotitis	mumps
monilia	thrush
nasal congestion	the nose is blocked (up), bunged up, a stuffy nose, stuffed up nose
nasal discharge, mucus	snot (*v.*), boogies (*v.*), snotters (*v.*)
running nose	runny nose
peritonsillar abscess	quinsy
tinnitus	ringing in the ears
vertigo	dizziness, to feel dizzy
Mouth	
abscess	gumboil
caries	tooth decay
dental cavity (carious defect or lesion)	cavity
extraction	to have a tooth taken out, removed, pulled
halitosis	bad breath
gingiva	gum
maxilla	upper jaw
mandible	lower jaw
palate	roof of the mouth
Skin	
alopecia	baldness, to be bald, thin on top
comedone	blackhead
contusion	bruise, the skin is bruised, goose-egg
furuncle	boil
herpes simplex	cold sore
seborrhea	scurf
pellagra	rough skin, scales/scaly skin
pruritus	itch, to be/feel itchy
herpes zoster	shingles
tinea	ringworm
ringworm (of the feet)	athlete's foot
scabies	the itch
sudor	sweat
sudamen	sweat blister, prickly heat
urticaria	nettle rash, hives, heat spots
verruca	wart
Bones and Joints	
bursitis	housemaid's knee (can be in other places, e.g., elbow)
rachitis	rickets
subluxation	dislocation
hernia	rupture
thorax	chest
talipes	club foot, to be club-footed
tenosynovitis	inflamed tendons
spine	backbone
ankylosing spondylitis	bamboo spine, bow legs/bandy legs

Medical Description	General Description
Heart and Lungs	
arteriosclerosis	hardening of the arteries
coronary thrombosis	heart attack
hypotension	low blood pressure
hypertension	high blood pressure
myocardial infarction	heart attack
pertussis	whooping cough
tachycardia	palpitations, heart flutters
tuberculosis	TB, consumption
trachea	windpipe, thrapple (Scots)
Gastro-Intestinal System	
colic	gripes
dyspepsia	indigestion, upset stomach
flatulence	to belch, to burp, to fart (*v.*), to let a fart (*v.*), to break wind, to let one fly (*v.*), to cut the cheese (U.S. [*v.*])
pyrosis	heartburn
obese	fat
stomach	guts, belly, tummy
recurrent appendicitis	grumbling appendix
vomiting	to bring it up, to puke, to throw up, to heave, heaves, to be sick, to barf (US), boak (Scots [*v.*]), spew, retch
dry	
Excretory System	
anus	arse (*v.*), ass (US [*v.*])
buttocks	arse (*v.*), ass (US [*v.*]), bottom, bum (*v.*), back side, rear, behind, seat, fanny (US [*v.*])
costive	to be constipated, stopped up
diarrhea	to have the runs, the trots, loose bowels, the shits (*v.*), Deli belly, Montezuma's revenge
enuresis	bed wetting, to wet the bed
incontinence	cannot hold one's water
feces, stools	shit (*v.*), crap (*v.*), shite (*v.*)
to micturate, urinate	to take a leak (*v.*), go to the john, pass water, pee (*v.*), piss (*v.*), take a piss (*v.*), do a number one (*v.*) wee-wee (child), pee-pee (child)
hemorrhoids	piles
infective hepatitis	catarrhal jaundice
nephritis	Bright's disease
tenesmus	straining
to open one's bowels	to do a number two, shit (*v.*), take a crap (*v.*), crap (*v.*), drop a brick (*v.*), a log(*v.*), to dump (*v.*)
Reproductive System	
dilation and curettage	a D. and C., a scrape
dysmenorrhea	period pains, cramps
menopause	the change of life
genitals	private parts, privates, goolies (*v.*)
leucorrhea	whites, discharge
obstetrics	midwifery
placenta	the afterbirth
parturition	to be in labor
uterus	womb
prepuce	foreskin

Medical Description	General Description
Sex/Sexual Anatomy	
condom	French letter, a rubber (US [v.]), Johnny (v.), durex, skin, raincoat (US [v.]), sheath
genitals	private parts, privates, down below
penis	privates, dick (v.), cock (v.), schlong (v.), dong (v.), prick (v.), willie (v.), tail (v.)
vagina	down below, private, up inside, cunt(v.), pussy (v.), quim (v.), jute (v.), twat (v.)
orgasm	climax, to come
sexual intercourse	to make love, to do it (v.), fuck (v.), screw (US [v.]), make it, bonk (v.), have it off (v.), bang (v.)
breasts	chest, bosom, boobs (v.), tits (v.), knockers (v.), a pair (v.)
testicles	balls (v.), bollocks (v.), nuts (v.), gonads (v.), goolies(v.)

Clinical Signs	
edema	dropsy
pyrexia	fever, temperature
syncope	fainting, to black out, pass out

Diseases of the Arteries and Blood	
erythema pernio	chilblains
thrombus	blood clot
Raynaud's disease	white or dead fingers
arterial (venous) thrombosis	white leg
hypoglycemia	low blood sugar

Around the Hospital	
analgesic	painkiller
sedative	sleeping pill, dope
drugs	medicine, dope
virus or bacteria	bug
sanitary towel	pads, STs, sanitary napkins
(her) condition has improved	(she) has got better, well again
WC	toilet, loo, gents, ladies, head, john, the wash room, bog(v.), bathroom
sleep	to snooze, to drop off, to get forty winks, to have/take a nap, doze, get some Zs

Diseases – Viral, Bacterial, Congenital	
brucellosis	undulant fever
chorea	St. Vitus Dance
cancer	a growth, the big C, tumor
herpes zoster	shingles
hydrophobia	rabies
infectious mononucleosis	glandular fever, the kissing disease
influenza	flu
lymphadenoma	Hodgkin's disease
poliomyelitis	infantile paralysis, polio
scarletina	scarlet fever
rubella	German measles
rubeola	measles
tetanus	lockjaw
varicella	chicken pox
variola	smallpox
diabetes mellitus	sugar

Medical Terminology

Medicine uses many specialized words. Learning them is a bit like learning a new language. Many of these words derive from Greek or Latin. In this section you will see the "building-blocks" of medical vocabulary and learn the key to recognizing many medical words. Note as well the syllable stress in medical words (italicized in the tables). This will help you to pronounce them correctly.

Word parts are often combined to form new, compound words. The tables below give examples of word parts that often appear at the beginning or end of medical terms. Many of the same "building blocks" can also be found in the middle of compound words.

1. Table of word beginnings in compound words

Word part	Meaning	Term
a-, an-	not, without	an*o*xia *ap*nea
ab-	away from	ab*duc*tion ab*nor*mal a*bor*tion
ad-	to, toward	ad*duc*tion ad*ner*val ad*re*nal gland
ante-	before	ante *ci*bum ante*flex*ion ante*na*tal
anti-	against, counter	antibi*o*tic *an*tibody *an*tigen antipyo*gen*ic anti*sep*tic anti*tox*in
arter(i)-	artery	arterioscle*ro*sis

119

Word part	Meaning	Term
aur-	ear	au*ric*ular auri*nas*al
auto-	self	au*to*logous auto*nom*ic auto*ser*um
bi-	two	bifur*ca*tion bi*lat*eral bi*lo*bate
blast-	bud, cell	blas*to*ma *blast*ula
brady-	slow	brady*car*dia
bronch-	windpipe	bron*chi*tis bron*chos*copy
carcin-	crab, cancer	carci*no*ma
cardi-	heart	*car*diac car*di*tis
cata-	down	cat*a*bolism cata*ton*ic
con-	with, together	con*nec*tive con*gen*ital con*trac*tion
contra-	against, counter	contra*cep*tive contraindi*ca*tion
crani(o)-	skull	cranioscle*ro*sis
de-	down, from, lack of	decompo*si*tion dehy*dra*tion
derm(at)-	skin	derma*to*logy
dia-	through, apart	diag*no*sis diar*rhe*a
digit-	finger	*dig*ital
dys-	bad, painful	dys*pha*sia *dys*trophy

Word part	Meaning	Term
ec(to)-	extra, outside	ec*cen*tric *ect*oderm *ect*oplasm
en(do)-	in, within	*end*ocrine *end*oderm endo*met*riosis
enter(o)-	intestine	ente*ri*tis enterocen*te*sis
epi-	in addition to, upon	epi*glott*is epi*the*lium
eu-	good, normal	eu*peps*ia eup*ne*a
ex(o)-	out, outside	ex*cre*tion exo*path*ic
faci-	face	facio*lin*gual
fibr-	fiber	fib*ro*ma
hemi-	half	hemiglos*sec*tomy
hepat-	liver	he*pat*ic hepa*ti*tis
hyper-	above, beyond	hyper*pla*sia *hy*pertension hy*per*trophy
hypo-	deficient, below	hypogly*ce*mia hypo*ten*sion
hyster(o)-	womb	hyste*rec*tomy *hys*terospasm
in-	not	in*som*niac in*va*lid
in-	in, on	in*ci*sion in*ser*tion
infra-	beneath, inferior	infra*ster*nal
inter-	among, between	inter*cos*tal
intra-	within	intra*ve*nous

Word part	Meaning	Term
kerat-	horn, cornea	kera*to*lysis
lapar-	flank	lapa*ro*tomy
lact-	milk	lacto*glob*ulin
linguo-	tongue	linguo*gingi*val
macro-	large	macroce*phal*ic
mal-	bad	mal*func*tion mal*ig*nant
mes(o)-	middle	*mes*oderm
meta-	beyond, accompanying change	meta*mor*phosis meta*sta*sis
micro-	small	*mi*crophage *mi*croscope
pan-	all	pana*cea* panarth*ri*tis
para-	beside, beyond	pa*ral*ysis
per-	through	per*fu*sion
peri-	around	peri*car*dium peri*ph*ery
pod-	foot	po*di*atry
poly-	many	poly*sper*mia
post-	after, behind	post*na*tal pos*to*ral
pre-	before, in front of	pre*na*tal
pro-	before	*pro*lapse
pseudo-	false	pseudopara*ple*gia
re-	again	re*mis*sion re*trac*tion
retro-	behind, back	retroperito*ne*al
semi-	half	semi*con*scious
sub-	under	sub*lum*bar

Word part	Meaning	Term
super-	above, beyond	supermo*til*ity
supra-	above	supra*re*nal glands
sym-, syn-	with, together	symbi*osis* sympa*thetic* *syn*drome
tachy-	fast	tachy*car*dia
tox-	poison	tox*e*mia
trans-	across	trans*fu*sion
traumato-	wound	trauma*to*pathy
ultra-	beyond	ultra*son*ic
vas-	vessel	*vas*cular

2. Table of word endings in compound words

Word part	Meaning	Term
-centesis	puncture	amniocen*tes*is paracen*tes*is
-clysis	washing	entero*cl*ysis
-ectasis	stretching, dilation	angie*c*tasis
-emesis	vomiting	hema*tem*esis hyper*em*esis
-genesis	production	carcino*gen*esis dys*gen*esis
-iasis	condition, formation of	li*thi*asis pso*ri*asis
-itis	inflammation	arth*ri*tis car*di*tis ente*ri*tis
-lysis	destruction	ana*ly*sis di*al*ysis hepa*tol*ysis

Word part	*Meaning*	*Term*
-osis	diseased condition	anky*lo*sis derma*to*sis lymphocy*to*sis
-pepsia	digestion	dys*pep*sia
-phagia	eating, swallowing	dys*phag*ia poly*phag*ia
-plasty	surgical repair	pa*la*toplasty
-ptosis	falling	blepharop*to*sis gastrop*to*sis nephrop*to*sis
-ptysis	splitting	he*mop*tysis
-rhage, -rhagia	bursting forth of blood	gastror*rhag*ia *hem*orrhage
-rhea	flow, discharge	rhinor*rhe*a
-rhexis	rupture	angior*rhex*is cardior*rhex*is hysteror*rhex*is
-sclerosis	hardening	arterioscle*ro*sis nephroscle*ro*sis otoscle*ro*sis
-spasm	sudden, violent contraction of muscles	py*lo*rospasm
-stalsis	contraction	peri*stal*sis
-statis	stopping, controlling	chole*ta*sis
-stenosis	tightening, stricture	enteroste*no*sis

Describing the Body

Look at these combining words and adjectives, which are used in medical terminology to describe the body, its organs, and body functions.

-cephal- head
(encephalograph)

ophthalm- eye
(opthalmology)

rhin- nose
(rhinitis)

phac- eye lens
(phacosclerosis)

crani- head
(craniometry)

or- mouth
(intraoral)

bucc- cheek
(distobuccal)

ot- ear
(parotid)

dent- tooth
(dental)

prosop- face
(diprosopus)

thyr- thyroid
(thyrocricotomy)

phren- mind
(schizophrenia)

phob- fear
(claustrophobia)

audi- ear
(auditory)

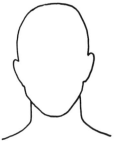

odont- tooth
(orthodontia)

aur- ear
(aurinasal)

cerebro- brain
(cerebrospinal)

nas- nose
(palatonasal)

pil- hair
(pilation)

sial- saliva
(polysialia)

laryng- windpipe
(laryngendoscope)

trich- hair
(trichoid)

aden- gland
(adenoma/adenoid)

ment- mind
(dementia)

psych- mind, soul
(psychosomatic)

faci- face
(brachiofaciolingual)

front- forehead
(nasofrontal)

gloss- tongue
(trichoglossia)

glott- tongue, larynx
(glottic)

cheil- lip
(cheiloschisis)

blephar- eyelid
(blepharitis)

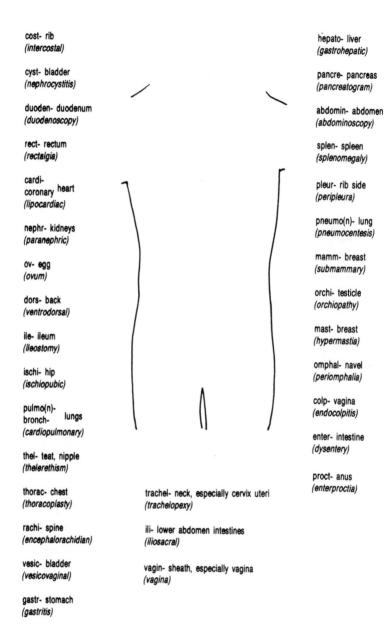

cost- rib
(intercostal)

cyst- bladder
(nephrocystitis)

duoden- duodenum
(duodenoscopy)

rect- rectum
(rectalgia)

cardi-
coronary heart
(lipocardiac)

nephr- kidneys
(paranephric)

ov- egg
(ovum)

dors- back
(ventrodorsal)

ile- ileum
(ileostomy)

ischi- hip
(ischiopubic)

pulmo(n)-
bronch- lungs
(cardiopulmonary)

thel- teat, nipple
(thelerethism)

thorac- chest
(thoracoplasty)

rachi- spine
(encephalorachidian)

vesic- bladder
(vesicovaginal)

gastr- stomach
(gastritis)

hepato- liver
(gastrohepatic)

pancre- pancreas
(pancreatogram)

abdomin- abdomen
(abdominoscopy)

splen- spleen
(splenomegaly)

pleur- rib side
(peripleura)

pneumo(n)- lung
(pneumocentesis)

mamm- breast
(submammary)

orchi- testicle
(orchiopathy)

mast- breast
(hypermastia)

omphal- navel
(periomphalia)

colp- vagina
(endocolpitis)

enter- intestine
(dysentery)

proct- anus
(enterproctia)

trachel- neck, especially cervix uteri
(trachelopexy)

ili- lower abdomen intestines
(iliosacral)

vagin- sheath, especially vagina
(vagina)

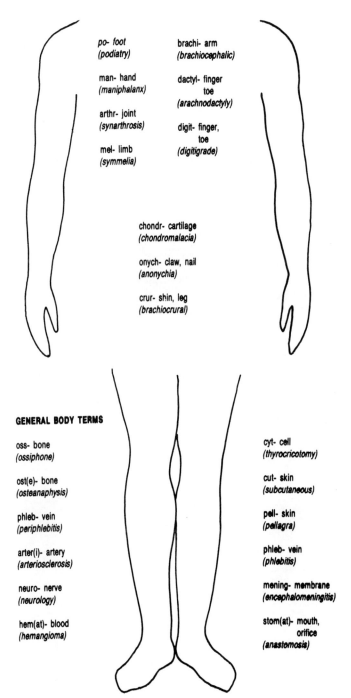

po- foot
(podiatry)

man- hand
(maniphalanx)

arthr- joint
(synarthrosis)

mel- limb
(symmelia)

brachi- arm
(brachiocephalic)

dactyl- finger
toe
(arachnodactyly)

digit- finger,
toe
(digitigrade)

chondr- cartilage
(chondromalacia)

onych- claw, nail
(anonychia)

crur- shin, leg
(brachiocrural)

GENERAL BODY TERMS

oss- bone
(ossiphone)

ost(e)- bone
(osteanaphysis)

phleb- vein
(periphlebitis)

arter(i)- artery
(arteriosclerosis)

neuro- nerve
(neurology)

hem(at)- blood
(hemangioma)

cyt- cell
(thyrocricotomy)

cut- skin
(subcutaneous)

pell- skin
(pellagra)

phleb- vein
(phlebitis)

mening- membrane
(encephalomeningitis)

stom(at)- mouth,
orifice
(anastomosis)

Medical Terms for Parts of the Body

Look at these combining words and adjectives, which are used to describe parts of the body and its organs.

1.	head	-cephalo
2.	eye	ophthalmo-
3.	nose	rhino-
4.	ear	aur(i)-, ot(o)-
5.	neck	cervico-
6.	lip	cheilo-
7.	hand	chiro-
8.	finger, toe	dactylo-
9.	skin	dermo-
10.	skull	cranio-
11.	nerve	neuro-
12.	brain	cerebro-
13.	blood	hemo-
14.	rib	costo-
15.	liver	hepato-
16.	lungs	pulmonary, bronchial
17.	pancreas	pancreatic
18.	thyroid gland	thyroid
19.	cell	cyto-
20.	bone	osteo-
21.	intestine	intestinal
22.	bladder	cysto-
23.	uterus	metro-
24.	duodenum	duodenal
25.	rectum	rectal
26.	heart	cardio-, cardiac, coronary
27.	vessel	angio-
28.	gland	adeno-
29.	stomach	gastro-
30.	joint	arthro-
31.	kidneys	nephro-

Equivalents and Conversion

Fahrenheit		Centigrade
212	Boiling Point	100
194		90
176		80
158		70
140		60
122		50
104		40
86		30
68		20
50		10
32	Freezing Point	0
14		-10
0		-17.8

To convert *Fahrenheit* temperature into *Centigrade*: subtract 32 and multiply by 5/9 (five-ninths).

To convert *Centigrade* temperature into *Fahrenheit*: multiply by 9/5 (nine-fifths) and add 32.

CONVERSION TABLES FOR MEASUREMENT

Metric		Britain and USA
Length		
10 millimeters (mm)	1 centimeter (cm)	0.393 inches (in)
100 centimeters	1 meter (m)	39.37 in or 1.094 yards
1,000 meters	1 kilometer (km)	0.621 miles (about 2/3 mile)
Weight		
10 milligrams (mg)	1 centigram (cg)	0.154 grains
100 centigrams	1 gram (g)	15.432 grains
1,000 grams	1 kilogram (kg)	2.204 pounds
1,000 kilograms	1 tonne	19.684 hundredweight
Fluid measure		
10 milliliters (ml)	1 centiliter (cl)	0.338 fluid ounce
100 centiliters	1 liter	1.057 quarts

129

	Britain and USA	Metric
Weight		
16 drams (dr)	1 ounce (oz.)	28.35 grams
16 ounces	1 pound (lb.)	0.454 kilograms
14 pounds	1 stone	6.356 kilograms
2 stone	1 quarter	12.7 kilograms
4 quarters	1 hundredweight (cwt)	50.8 kilograms
112 pounds	1 cwt	50.8 kilograms
20 cwt	1 ton	1,016.04 kilograms

	USA	Metric
Fluid measure		
4 gills	1 pint	0.473 liters
2 pints	1 quart	0.946 liters
4 quarts	1 gallon	3.785 liters

Numerical Expressions:
A Guide to Pronunciation

Below are some symbols and expressions used in ordinary measurement, in mathematics, in statistics, and in combination with SI units. (SI = *Système International d'Unités*, a system of units, e.g., meters, kilograms, seconds, etc., adopted in 1960 by an international committee of scientists.) Expressions in brackets tend to be less formal or technical than the ones given immediately. Sometimes examples are given in parentheses.

Symbols

+	plus
−	minus
±	plus or minus (approximately)
×	(is) multiplied by (times)
÷	(is) divided by
=	equals
≠	is not equal to (does not equal)
≅	is approximately equal to
≡	is equivalent to (is identical with)
<	is less than (e.g., < 0.3 = less than zero point three)
≮	is not less than
>	is more than (e.g., > 8.0 = more than eight point zero)
≯	is not more than
≥	is more than or equal to
%	percent
∞	infinity
↑	increases
↓	decreases
√	square root
x^2	x squared
x^3	x cubed
x^4	x to the power four (e.g., 3×10^9/three times ten to the power of nine; you could also say: "ten to the ninth")

Numbers

374	three hundred seventy-four
4,678	four thousand six hundred seventy-eight
7,042	seven thousand forty-two
52.1	fifty-two point one

28.39	twenty-eight point three nine
0	zero, nought
0.62	zero point six two
0.03	zero point zero three
$^1/_8$	an eighth, one-eighth
$^1/_4$	a quarter, one-quarter, a fourth
$^1/_3$	a third, one-third
$^1/_2$	a half, one-half
$^3/_4$	three-quarters
$^{13}/_{20}$	thirteen over twenty, thirteen-twentieths
c. 30	about thirty
1:7	one to seven

Time

2:55	two fifty-five, five to three (five of three)
3:30	three thirty, half past three, half three
4:10	four ten, ten past four (ten after four)
6:45	six forty five, a quarter to seven (a quarter of seven)
7:15	seven fifteen, a quarter past seven (a quarter after seven [US])
8:00	eight o'clock (eight a.m., eight p.m.)

Years

1900	nineteen hundred
1905	nineteen oh five
1987	nineteen eighty-seven
2000	two thousand

Temperature

25.2°C	twenty-five point two degrees Centigrade (Celsius)
43°F	forty-three degrees Fahrenheit

Other Measurements

90.40 mmHg	ninety over forty millimeters of mercury
mmol/l	millimoles per liter
l/min	liters per minute
m^2	square meter(s), meter squared
sq.m	square meter
H_2	H two
HCO_3	H-C-O three

Vocabulary Checklist

A selected list of key words used in medical communication is given here. The list contains both technical and nontechnical vocabulary and is designed to give you the opportunity to test your knowledge and revise some important vocabulary in English. Check any unknown words in the dictionary and tick the box ☑ when you think you have understood the meaning of the word.

A

- [ ] abcess
- [ ] abdomen
- [ ] abnormal
- [ ] abnormality
- [ ] abortion
- [ ] abrasion
- [ ] absence
- [ ] absolute
- [ ] absorption
- [ ] accelerate
- [ ] accident
- [ ] accommodation
- [ ] accompany
- [ ] accumulate
- [ ] acetylcholine
- [ ] ache
- [ ] acid
- [ ] acidosis
- [ ] acidotic
- [ ] acquire
- [ ] acromegaly
- [ ] action
- [ ] activate
- [ ] activity
- [ ] acute
- [ ] additional
- [ ] adequate
- [ ] adhere
- [ ] adhesion
- [ ] adipose
- [ ] adjacent
- [ ] adjust
- [ ] administer
- [ ] administration
- [ ] admission
- [ ] admit

- [ ] adrenaline
- [ ] adult
- [ ] advance
- [ ] advantage
- [ ] advice
- [ ] advise
- [ ] aerobic
- [ ] aetiology, etiology
- [ ] afebrile
- [ ] afferent
- [ ] age
- [ ] agent
- [ ] aggravate
- [ ] agreement
- [ ] aid
- [ ] ailment
- [ ] aim
- [ ] air
- [ ] airway
- [ ] albumen
- [ ] alert
- [ ] alimentary
- [ ] alive
- [ ] alkalosis
- [ ] allergic
- [ ] allergy
- [ ] allow
- [ ] alter
- [ ] alveolar
- [ ] amalgam
- [ ] ambulance
- [ ] ambulant
- [ ] amenorrhoea
- [ ] amino acid
- [ ] amnesia
- [ ] amniocentesis
- [ ] amount

- [ ] amylase
- [ ] anaemia, anemia
- [ ] anaerobic
- [ ] anaesthesia, anesthesia
- [ ] analgesic
- [ ] analyse, analyze
- [ ] analysis
- [ ] anaphylaxis
- [ ] anaplasia
- [ ] anaplastic
- [ ] anastomosis
- [ ] anatomy
- [ ] aneurysm
- [ ] angina
- [ ] angiogram
- [ ] animal
- [ ] ankle
- [ ] ankylosing spondylitis
- [ ] annual
- [ ] anomalous
- [ ] anorexia
- [ ] another
- [ ] anoxaemia, anoxemia
- [ ] anoxia
- [ ] antenatal
- [ ] anterior
- [ ] antibiotic
- [ ] antibody
- [ ] anticoagulant
- [ ] antigen
- [ ] antihistamine
- [ ] antitussive
- [ ] antiseptic
- [ ] anuria
- [ ] anus
- [ ] anxiety
- [ ] aorta

☐ apathy
☐ apnoea, apnea
☐ apparent
☐ appear
☐ appearance
☐ appendectomy
☐ appendix
☐ appetite
☐ application
☐ apply
☐ appointment
☐ approach
☐ approximately
☐ area
☐ arise
☐ arm
☐ armpit
☐ arrange
☐ arrest
☐ arrythmia
☐ arteriosclerosis
☐ artery
☐ arthrodesis
☐ article

☐ artificial
☐ ascend
☐ ascending colon
☐ ascites
☐ asphyxia
☐ aspiration
☐ aspirin
☐ assay
☐ associated
☐ assume
☐ asthenic
☐ asthma
☐ atelectasis
☐ atrial
☐ atrioventricular
☐ atrophy
☐ attack
☐ attain
☐ attempt
☐ attend
☐ attention
☐ attitude
☐ attribute
☐ atypical

☐ auriscope
☐ auscultation
☐ autistic
☐ autoclave
☐ autonomic
☐ autopsy
☐ available
☐ average
☐ avoid
☐ aware

B

☐ bacillus
☐ back
☐ bacteria
☐ bactericidal
☐ bad
☐ bandage
☐ bare
☐ barium enema
☐ basal
☐ base
☐ basic

☐ basis
☐ basophil
☐ bath
☐ bear
☐ beat
☐ bed
☐ bed-bath
☐ bed-cradle
☐ bedpan
☐ bedside
☐ behaviour, behavior

☐ benefit
☐ benign
☐ beta blocker
☐ bicarbonate
☐ bilateral
☐ bile
☐ bilirubin
☐ binary
☐ biopsy
☐ birth
☐ bitter

- [ ] bladder
- [ ] bleeding
- [ ] blind
- [ ] block
- [ ] blood
- [ ] blood bank
- [ ] blood cell
- [ ] blood circulation
- [ ] blood clot
- [ ] blood corpuscle
- [ ] blood culture
- [ ] blood flow
- [ ] blood group
- [ ] blood sugar level
- [ ] blood supply
- [ ] blood typing
- [ ] body

- [ ] boil
- [ ] bond
- [ ] bone
- [ ] bone marrow
- [ ] borderline
- [ ] born
- [ ] bottle
- [ ] botulism
- [ ] bowel
- [ ] brain
- [ ] branch
- [ ] break
- [ ] breast
- [ ] breastbone
- [ ] breath
- [ ] breathe
- [ ] breathlessness

- [ ] breed
- [ ] brief
- [ ] bronchitis
- [ ] bronchoscope
- [ ] bruise
- [ ] buccal
- [ ] bud
- [ ] buffer
- [ ] bundle
- [ ] burn
- [ ] burning
- [ ] bursitis
- [ ] buttock
- [ ] by-pass

C

- [ ] °C
- [ ] cadaver
- [ ] caecum, cecum
- [ ] caesarian, cesarian
- [ ] calcification
- [ ] calculus
- [ ] calf
- [ ] call
- [ ] calm
- [ ] canal
- [ ] cancer
- [ ] capacity
- [ ] carbohydrate
- [ ] carbon dioxide
- [ ] carcinoma
- [ ] card
- [ ] cardiac
- [ ] cardiomegaly

- [ ] cardiovascular
- [ ] care
- [ ] caries
- [ ] carry
- [ ] cartilage
- [ ] cartilaginous
- [ ] catabolism
- [ ] catatonia
- [ ] catatonic
- [ ] catch
- [ ] catching
- [ ] catecholamine
- [ ] catheter
- [ ] catheterization
- [ ] CAT scan (CT scan)
- [ ] causative agent
- [ ] cause
- [ ] cavity

- [ ] cease
- [ ] cell
- [ ] centrifuge
- [ ] cerebellum
- [ ] cerebral
- [ ] cerebrospinal fluid
- [ ] cerebrovascular accident
- [ ] cervical
- [ ] cervix
- [ ] cessation
- [ ] challenge
- [ ] chamber
- [ ] change
- [ ] characteristic
- [ ] chart
- [ ] chemist
- [ ] chemotherapy
- [ ] chest

☐ chickenpox	☐ common	☐ contagious
☐ child	☐ complain	☐ contain
☐ chill	☐ complaint	☐ contamination
☐ choice	☐ complete	☐ contents
☐ choke	☐ complicate	☐ continuous
☐ cholelithiasis	☐ complication	☐ contract
☐ cholesterol	☐ composed	☐ contraction
☐ chorionic villi	☐ compound	☐ contraceptive
☐ chronic	☐ compulsion	☐ contribute
☐ ciliary	☐ computed axial tomography	☐ control
☐ circulation	☐ concave	☐ contusion
☐ circulatory	☐ concentration	☐ convalescence
☐ circumstance	☐ concerned	☐ convalescent
☐ cirrhosis	☐ concerning	☐ convenient
☐ clammy	☐ conclusion	☐ convex
☐ claustrophobia	☐ condition	☐ coordination
☐ cleanse	☐ confirm	☐ coronary
☐ clear	☐ confused	☐ corpse
☐ clearance	☐ congenital	☐ corpuscle
☐ clinic	☐ congestion	☐ correct
☐ clinical	☐ congestive	☐ correlate
☐ close	☐ conjunctiva	☐ correspond
☐ closure	☐ connection	☐ corticosteroid
☐ clot	☐ conscious	☐ cough
☐ coagulation	☐ consciousness	☐ count
☐ coarctation	☐ consequently	☐ course
☐ coeliac, celiac	☐ consider	☐ cover
☐ coil	☐ considerable	☐ cramp
☐ cold	☐ consist	☐ cranial
☐ collagen	☐ consistent	☐ creatinine
☐ collect	☐ consolidation	☐ crepitation
☐ colon	☐ constant	☐ crisis
☐ colour	☐ constipation	☐ critical
☐ colporrhaphy	☐ constitute	☐ cross-infection
☐ combat	☐ constriction	☐ crutch
☐ combine	☐ consult	☐ culture
☐ comfortable	☐ consultant	☐ curable

- [ ] cure
- [ ] current
- [ ] cut
- [ ] cutaneous
- [ ] cuticle

- [ ] cyanosis
- [ ] cyclothymic
- [ ] cyst
- [ ] cystic fibrosis
- [ ] cystitis

- [ ] cytological
- [ ] cytoscope
- [ ] cytoscopy

D

- [ ] daily
- [ ] damage
- [ ] dangerous
- [ ] data
- [ ] dead
- [ ] deaf
- [ ] decide
- [ ] decline
- [ ] decrease
- [ ] deep
- [ ] defaecation, defecation
- [ ] defect
- [ ] deficiency
- [ ] define
- [ ] definite
- [ ] definitive
- [ ] degeneration
- [ ] degree
- [ ] dehydrated
- [ ] delay
- [ ] delicate
- [ ] delirium
- [ ] delivery
- [ ] delusion
- [ ] demand
- [ ] dementia
- [ ] demise
- [ ] demonstrate
- [ ] demulcent
- [ ] demyelinating

- [ ] dense
- [ ] department
- [ ] depend
- [ ] deposit
- [ ] depression
- [ ] deprive
- [ ] deprivation
- [ ] dermatitis
- [ ] dermatology
- [ ] describe
- [ ] destroy
- [ ] detect
- [ ] deteriorate
- [ ] determine
- [ ] develop
- [ ] development
- [ ] deviation
- [ ] diabetes insipidus
- [ ] diabetes mellitus
- [ ] diagnose
- [ ] diagnosis
- [ ] diaphragm
- [ ] diaphragmatic
- [ ] diarrhoea, diarrhea
- [ ] diastolic
- [ ] diazepam
- [ ] die
- [ ] diet
- [ ] difference
- [ ] differential

- [ ] differentiate
- [ ] difficulty
- [ ] diffuse
- [ ] digestion
- [ ] digitalise
- [ ] digoxin
- [ ] dilate
- [ ] dilution
- [ ] diminish
- [ ] disappear
- [ ] discharge
- [ ] disclose
- [ ] discomfort
- [ ] discontinue
- [ ] discover
- [ ] discuss
- [ ] disease
- [ ] disinfect
- [ ] disorder
- [ ] displacement
- [ ] dissection
- [ ] disseminate
- [ ] distal
- [ ] distension
- [ ] distinguish
- [ ] distribution
- [ ] disturbance
- [ ] diuretic
- [ ] diverticular
- [ ] divide

- [ ] dizziness
- [ ] doctor
- [ ] dorsal
- [ ] dosage
- [ ] dose
- [ ] doubt
- [ ] drainage
- [ ] dressing
- [ ] drink
- [ ] drip

- [ ] drop
- [ ] drowsy
- [ ] drug
- [ ] dry
- [ ] duct
- [ ] dull
- [ ] dullness
- [ ] duodenum
- [ ] duration
- [ ] during

- [ ] duty
- [ ] dwarfism
- [ ] dye
- [ ] dysentery
- [ ] dysfunction
- [ ] dyspareunia
- [ ] dysphagia
- [ ] dyspnoea, dyspnea
- [ ] dystocia
- [ ] dysuria

E

- [ ] ear
- [ ] early
- [ ] ecchymosis
- [ ] eczema
- [ ] eczematous
- [ ] effect
- [ ] effective
- [ ] efferent
- [ ] efficiency
- [ ] effort
- [ ] effusion
- [ ] elated
- [ ] elbow
- [ ] elderly
- [ ] electrocardiogram
- [ ] electroconvulsive therapy
- [ ] electroencephalogram
- [ ] elevate
- [ ] eliminate
- [ ] emboli
- [ ] embolism
- [ ] embryo
- [ ] embryonic
- [ ] emergency
- [ ] emesis

- [ ] emotion
- [ ] emphysema
- [ ] employ
- [ ] employment
- [ ] empty
- [ ] empyema
- [ ] encounter
- [ ] endemic
- [ ] emdocrine
- [ ] endoplasm
- [ ] endothelium
- [ ] endotracheal
- [ ] endure
- [ ] enema
- [ ] engulf
- [ ] enlarge
- [ ] enlargement
- [ ] ENT
- [ ] enteric fever
- [ ] enteritis
- [ ] entrance
- [ ] environment
- [ ] enzyme
- [ ] eosinophil
- [ ] epidemiology

- [ ] epididymo-orchitis
- [ ] epiphysis
- [ ] equal
- [ ] equipment
- [ ] erosion
- [ ] error
- [ ] erythema
- [ ] erythrocyte
- [ ] eruption
- [ ] erythrocyte sediment-ation rate
- [ ] erythrocytic
- [ ] essential
- [ ] establish
- [ ] estimate
- [ ] ether
- [ ] euthyroid
- [ ] evacuate
- [ ] evacuation
- [ ] evaluate
- [ ] event
- [ ] evidence
- [ ] evident
- [ ] exact
- [ ] exaggerated
- [ ] examination

- [ ] examine
- [ ] excavate
- [ ] except
- [ ] excess
- [ ] excessive
- [ ] exchange
- [ ] excision
- [ ] excited
- [ ] exclude
- [ ] excreta
- [ ] excretion

- [ ] exercise
- [ ] exertion
- [ ] exophthalmos
- [ ] expectoration
- [ ] experience
- [ ] expiration
- [ ] explain
- [ ] exploration
- [ ] exploratory
- [ ] explosive
- [ ] exposure

- [ ] extend
- [ ] extensive
- [ ] extent
- [ ] external
- [ ] extract
- [ ] extremely
- [ ] extremity
- [ ] exudate
- [ ] eye
- [ ] eyeball
- [ ] eyelid

F

- [ ] fistula-in-ano
- [ ] fit
- [ ] fix
- [ ] flaccid
- [ ] flatus
- [ ] flow
- [ ] fluid
- [ ] flush
- [ ] flutter

- [ ] focus
- [ ] follow-up
- [ ] food
- [ ] foot
- [ ] forceps
- [ ] forearm
- [ ] forehead
- [ ] foreign
- [ ] foreign body

- [ ] fracture
- [ ] fragile
- [ ] free
- [ ] frequency
- [ ] frequent
- [ ] function
- [ ] fundus
- [ ] funduscopy
- [ ] furuncle

G

- [ ] gag
- [ ] gain
- [ ] gall
- [ ] gallbladder
- [ ] gammaglobulin
- [ ] gargle
- [ ] gastric
- [ ] gauze
- [ ] gene
- [ ] general
- [ ] generalised
- [ ] generally
- [ ] genetic

- [ ] genital
- [ ] gentian violet
- [ ] geriatrics
- [ ] germ
- [ ] gestation
- [ ] giardiasis
- [ ] giddiness
- [ ] gigantism
- [ ] gland
- [ ] glandular
- [ ] glomerulonephritis
- [ ] glottis
- [ ] glove

- [ ] glucose
- [ ] glycogen
- [ ] glycosuria
- [ ] goitre, goiter
- [ ] gonorrhoea, gonorrhe
- [ ] gout
- [ ] gouty tophi
- [ ] gown
- [ ] grab rail
- [ ] grade
- [ ] gradually
- [ ] granule

☐ grave   ☐ grow   ☐ gut
☐ gravity   ☐ growth   ☐ gynaecology, gynecology
☐ graze   ☐ guinea-pig
☐ groin   ☐ gum

H

☐ haematemesis, hematemesis   ☐ heart sounds
☐ haematogenous, hematogenous   ☐ heat
☐ heamatology, hematology   ☐ heavy
☐ haematuria, hematuria   ☐ height
☐ haemoglogin, hemoglobin   ☐ help
☐ haemolytic, hemolytic   ☐ hemiparesis
☐ haemopoiesis, hemopoiesis   ☐ hemiplegia
☐ haemoptysis, hemoptysis   ☐ hepatic
☐ haemorrhage, hemorrhage   ☐ hepatitis
☐ haemorrhoids, hemorrhoids(us)   ☐ hepatocellular
☐ haemostasis, hemostasis   ☐ hereditary
☐ haemothorax, hemothorax   ☐ heredity
☐ hair   ☐ hernia
☐ hallucination   ☐ hiatus hernia
☐ hand   ☐ high
☐ handicapped   ☐ hilum
☐ happen   ☐ hip
☐ hard   ☐ hirsutism
☐ hazard   ☐ histology
☐ head   ☐ history
☐ headache   ☐ hoarse
☐ heal   ☐ home
☐ healing   ☐ homeostasis
☐ health   ☐ hormonal
☐ healthy   ☐ hormone
☐ hearing   ☐ hospital
☐ heart   ☐ hospitalize
☐ heartbeat   ☐ host
☐ heartburn   ☐ hot-water bottle
☐ heart failure   ☐ hour
☐ heart murmur   ☐ human

Vocabulary Checklist

- [ ] hunger
- [ ] hurt
- [ ] hydatidiform
- [ ] hydrochloric acid
- [ ] hydrocortisone
- [ ] hyperemesis
- [ ] hyperpnoea, hyperpnea
- [ ] hyperpyrexia
- [ ] hypertension

- [ ] hyperthyroidism
- [ ] hypertrophy
- [ ] hyperventilation
- [ ] hypnosis
- [ ] hypochondriacal
- [ ] hypochromic
- [ ] hypogammaglobulinaemia, hypogammaglobulinemia
- [ ] hypophyseal
- [ ] hypophysis

- [ ] hypotension
- [ ] hypothalamus
- [ ] hypothyroidism
- [ ] hypoxia
- [ ] hysterectomy
- [ ] hysteria
- [ ] hysterical

I

- [ ] identify
- [ ] idiopathic
- [ ] ileum
- [ ] ileus
- [ ] ill
- [ ] illness
- [ ] immediate
- [ ] immerse
- [ ] immobilization
- [ ] immunity
- [ ] immunize
- [ ] immunosupression
- [ ] impair
- [ ] impairment
- [ ] impotence
- [ ] improve
- [ ] incidence
- [ ] incipient
- [ ] incision
- [ ] incontinence
- [ ] increase
- [ ] incubation
- [ ] independent
- [ ] indicate
- [ ] indication
- [ ] indigestion

- [ ] individual
- [ ] induce
- [ ] induration
- [ ] infant
- [ ] infarction
- [ ] infectious
- [ ] inflame
- [ ] inflammation
- [ ] influence
- [ ] influenza
- [ ] information
- [ ] infusion
- [ ] inhale
- [ ] inherited
- [ ] inhibit
- [ ] inject
- [ ] injection
- [ ] injure
- [ ] injury
- [ ] in-patient
- [ ] insect
- [ ] insert
- [ ] insidious
- [ ] inspiration
- [ ] institution
- [ ] insufficiency

- [ ] insulin intake
- [ ] intense
- [ ] intensify
- [ ] intensity
- [ ] intensive care unit
- [ ] intercostal space
- [ ] interfere
- [ ] intermittent
- [ ] internal
- [ ] interrupt
- [ ] interstitial
- [ ] intervention
- [ ] intestinal
- [ ] intestine
- [ ] intolerable
- [ ] intoxication
- [ ] intramuscular
- [ ] intravenous
- [ ] intravenous pyelogram
- [ ] intubation
- [ ] invade
- [ ] invasion
- [ ] invasive
- [ ] investigate
- [ ] involve
- [ ] iodine

☐ iron
☐ irregular
☐ irreversible
☐ irrigate

☐ irritant
☐ irritation
☐ ischaemic, ischemic
☐ ischial

☐ isolate
☐ itch

J

☐ jaundice
☐ jaw
☐ jejunum
☐ join
☐ joint
☐ juice

K

☐ karyosome
☐ keto-acidosis
☐ ketones
☐ kidney
☐ kidney dish
☐ knee

☐ knowledge
☐ kyphoscoliosis

L

☐ labia
☐ laboratory
☐ labour, labor
☐ laceration
☐ lactate
☐ lactic acid
☐ laparotomy
☐ larynx
☐ late
☐ lateral
☐ laxative
☐ lay
☐ layer
☐ lay up
☐ leg
☐ length
☐ lesion
☐ lethargy
☐ leucocyte, leukocyte
☐ leucocytosis, leukocytosis
☐ level
☐ lie

☐ life
☐ life-threatening
☐ light
☐ limb
☐ limit
☐ lining
☐ lip
☐ lipase
☐ lipid
☐ list
☐ listen
☐ live
☐ liver
☐ living
☐ lobe
☐ lobotomy
☐ lobular
☐ localize
☐ locate
☐ long
☐ longevity
☐ longitudinal

☐ long-stay
☐ loop
☐ loose
☐ lose
☐ loss
☐ lotion
☐ low
☐ lower
☐ lozenge
☐ lumen
☐ lumbar
☐ lung
☐ lymph
☐ lymphodenopathy
☐ lymph node
☐ lymphocarcinoma

M

- [ ] macrocyte
- [ ] mactocytic
- [ ] macrophage
- [ ] macroscopic
- [ ] magnitude
- [ ] main
- [ ] maintain
- [ ] major
- [ ] majority
- [ ] malaise
- [ ] male
- [ ] malignant
- [ ] malnourished
- [ ] malnutrition
- [ ] management
- [ ] mania
- [ ] manic
- [ ] manifest
- [ ] manifestation
- [ ] manner
- [ ] manual
- [ ] margin
- [ ] mark
- [ ] marked
- [ ] masochism
- [ ] mass
- [ ] massive
- [ ] mature
- [ ] meal
- [ ] measles
- [ ] measure
- [ ] meatus
- [ ] medial
- [ ] mediastinum
- [ ] medical
- [ ] medication

- [ ] medicine
- [ ] medium
- [ ] melaena, melena
- [ ] melancholia
- [ ] melanoma
- [ ] member
- [ ] membrane
- [ ] menarche
- [ ] meningeal
- [ ] meningism
- [ ] meningitis
- [ ] menorrhagia
- [ ] mental
- [ ] mention
- [ ] metabolic
- [ ] metabolism
- [ ] metastasis
- [ ] metastatic
- [ ] microcytic
- [ ] micro-organism
- [ ] microscope
- [ ] microscopic
- [ ] middle
- [ ] mild
- [ ] mind
- [ ] minor
- [ ] minority
- [ ] mitral
- [ ] mix
- [ ] mixture
- [ ] mobility
- [ ] mode
- [ ] moderate
- [ ] mole
- [ ] monocyte
- [ ] month

- [ ] morbidity
- [ ] morphine
- [ ] mortality
- [ ] motile
- [ ] motility
- [ ] motion
- [ ] mouth
- [ ] movement
- [ ] mucosa
- [ ] mucus
- [ ] mucoid
- [ ] mucopurulent
- [ ] multiple
- [ ] multiply
- [ ] mumps
- [ ] murmur
- [ ] muscle
- [ ] musculoskeletal
- [ ] myalgia
- [ ] myelomatosis
- [ ] myocardial, infarction
- [ ] myxoedema, myxedema

N

- [ ] nail
- [ ] nasal
- [ ] natural
- [ ] nausea
- [ ] navel
- [ ] neck
- [ ] necropsy
- [ ] necrosis
- [ ] needle
- [ ] negative
- [ ] negligible
- [ ] neoplasm
- [ ] nerve
- [ ] nervous
- [ ] neuralgia
- [ ] neurasthenic
- [ ] neurology
- [ ] neuropathy
- [ ] neurosis
- [ ] neurotic
- [ ] neutralise, neutralize
- [ ] neutrophil
- [ ] newborn
- [ ] niacin
- [ ] nipple
- [ ] nocturnal
- [ ] node
- [ ] nodule
- [ ] noise
- [ ] normal
- [ ] nose
- [ ] note
- [ ] notice
- [ ] nourish
- [ ] nucleus
- [ ] nucleosis
- [ ] number
- [ ] numbness
- [ ] nurse
- [ ] nutrition
- [ ] nystagmus

O

- [ ] obese
- [ ] obscure
- [ ] observation
- [ ] observe
- [ ] obstetrics
- [ ] obstruction
- [ ] obtain
- [ ] obvious
- [ ] occasional
- [ ] occasionally
- [ ] occlusion
- [ ] occult
- [ ] occupational therapy
- [ ] occurrence
- [ ] odour, odor
- [ ] oedema, edema
- [ ] oesophagus, esophagus
- [ ] offspring
- [ ] ointment
- [ ] onset
- [ ] opening
- [ ] operate
- [ ] operation
- [ ] operative
- [ ] opiate
- [ ] opinion
- [ ] optimal
- [ ] oral
- [ ] orally
- [ ] organic
- [ ] organism
- [ ] orifice
- [ ] origin
- [ ] originate
- [ ] orthopaedics, orthopedics
- [ ] orthopnoea, orthopnea
- [ ] osmosis
- [ ] outbreak
- [ ] outcome
- [ ] out-patient
- [ ] overstrain
- [ ] oxygen

P

- [ ] pacemaker
- [ ] pad
- [ ] paediatrics, pediatrics
- [ ] paedophilia, pedophilia
- [ ] pain
- [ ] painful
- [ ] painless
- [ ] palate
- [ ] pale

- palliative
- pallid
- palm
- palpable
- palpate
- palpitation
- pancreas
- paraesthesia, paresthesia
- paralyse, paralyze
- paralysis
- parasite
- parasympathetic
- parietal
- parenchyma
- parent
- parenterally
- paresis
- parietal
- paronychia
- part
- partial
- particle
- pass
- passage
- passive
- patch
- patent
- pathogen
- pathology
- patient
- pattern
- pelvis
- penetrate
- penicillin
- pepsinogen
- peptic ulcer
- peptide

- percentage
- percussion
- perforate
- perform
- period
- peripheral
- peristalsis
- peritoneum
- permanent
- permeability
- permeable
- permit
- pernicious anaemia, pernicious anemia
- persist
- persistent
- perspiration
- petechiae
- phaeochromocytoma, pheochromocytoma (US)
- phagocyte
- phagocytic
- phenomenon
- pharmacolgy
- phobic
- physical
- physician
- physiology
- physiotherapy
- picture
- pigment
- pineal
- pituitary
- plasma
- plaster
- platelet
- pleura
- pneumonia

- poisoning
- poliomyelitis
- pollution
- polycythaemia, polycythemia
- polyp
- poor
- popliteal
- population
- portion
- position
- positive
- possibility
- posterior
- postmortem
- postoperative
- postural
- potential
- pregnant
- preparation
- prepare
- prescribe
- prescription
- presence
- present
- preserve
- pressure
- prevent
- primary
- principal
- prior
- private
- probe
- procedure
- proceed
- proctoscope
- prodromal
- produce

☐ production
☐ productive
☐ profound
☐ profuse
☐ progressive
☐ prognosis
☐ prolong
☐ prolonged
☐ prominent
☐ propanolol
☐ prosthesis
☐ prosthetic
☐ protect

☐ protein
☐ proteinuria
☐ prothrombin
☐ prove
☐ provide
☐ proximal
☐ pseudocyst
☐ psoriasis
☐ ptosis
☐ pulmonary
☐ pulse
☐ pump
☐ puncture

☐ pupil
☐ pure
☐ purify
☐ purpura
☐ purulent
☐ pus
☐ pustule
☐ pylorus
☐ pyramid
☐ pyramidal
☐ pyrexia

Q

☐ quality
☐ quantity
☐ queasy

☐ question
☐ quiet

☐ quinsy
☐ Q wave

R

☐ radial
☐ radiate
☐ radiation
☐ radiography
☐ radiology
☐ radiotherapy
☐ raise
☐ râle
☐ range
☐ rapid
☐ rare
☐ rash
☐ rate
☐ ration
☐ raw
☐ reaction

☐ reception
☐ recognize
☐ record
☐ recover
☐ recovery
☐ rectum
☐ recur
☐ recurrence
☐ reduce
☐ refer
☐ reference
☐ reflex
☐ regimen
☐ region
☐ regular
☐ regurgitation

☐ rehabilitation
☐ release
☐ reliable
☐ relief
☐ relieve
☐ remedy
☐ removal
☐ remove
☐ renal
☐ renal dialysis
☐ repair
☐ replace
☐ reproduce
☐ reproduction
☐ require
☐ research

☐ resection
☐ resemble
☐ resistance
☐ respiration
☐ respiratory
☐ respond
☐ response
☐ rest
☐ restore

☐ result
☐ resuscitate
☐ retain
☐ retention
☐ reveal
☐ reticulocyte
☐ reticuloendothelial
☐ retina
☐ review

☐ rheumatoid arthritis
☐ rhinorrhoea, rhinorrhea
☐ rib
☐ ribbon gauze
☐ rise
☐ routine
☐ rub
☐ rupture

S

☐ sac
☐ sacral
☐ safe
☐ saline
☐ saliva
☐ salivary discharge
☐ salt
☐ sample
☐ sanatorium
☐ saphenous
☐ satisfactory
☐ saturation
☐ save
☐ scale
☐ scalpel
☐ scaly
☐ scaphoid
☐ scar
☐ scarlet fever
☐ scheme
☐ schizoid
☐ sciatica
☐ science
☐ scientific
☐ scrub
☐ scrub-up

☐ search
☐ secondary
☐ secrete
☐ section
☐ sedative
☐ sediment
☐ sedimentation rate
☐ segmentation
☐ seizure
☐ select
☐ senile
☐ sensistive
☐ sensitivity
☐ separate
☐ series
☐ serious
☐ serous
☐ serum
☐ service
☐ set
☐ severe
☐ severity
☐ sew
☐ sex
☐ shadow
☐ shape

☐ sharp
☐ shiver
☐ shock
☐ shortness of breath
☐ shoulder
☐ show
☐ shunt
☐ sibling
☐ sick
☐ sickness
☐ side
☐ side effect
☐ sight
☐ sigmoid
☐ sigmoidoscopy
☐ sign
☐ significant
☐ simultaneous
☐ similar
☐ sinus
☐ site
☐ situation
☐ size
☐ skin
☐ skull
☐ sleep

- [ ] sleepiness
- [ ] sleeplessness
- [ ] slight
- [ ] sluice
- [ ] smallpox
- [ ] smear
- [ ] smell
- [ ] smooth
- [ ] soiled
- [ ] solid
- [ ] soluble
- [ ] solution
- [ ] sore
- [ ] sound
- [ ] source
- [ ] space
- [ ] spasm
- [ ] species
- [ ] specimen
- [ ] speculum
- [ ] sphincter
- [ ] sphygmomanometer
- [ ] spina bifida
- [ ] spinal column
- [ ] spinal cord
- [ ] spine
- [ ] spiral
- [ ] spleen
- [ ] splint
- [ ] spondylolisthesis
- [ ] spontaneous
- [ ] sprain
- [ ] sputum
- [ ] squamous
- [ ] stage
- [ ] stain
- [ ] standard

- [ ] stasis
- [ ] state
- [ ] stay
- [ ] sterilize
- [ ] sternum
- [ ] stethoscope
- [ ] stiff
- [ ] stimulate
- [ ] stitch
- [ ] stomach
- [ ] stool
- [ ] strain
- [ ] stratified
- [ ] strength
- [ ] stress
- [ ] stretcher
- [ ] striated
- [ ] strip
- [ ] strong
- [ ] structure
- [ ] study
- [ ] sturdy
- [ ] subarachnoid
- [ ] subcutaneous
- [ ] subject
- [ ] subsequent
- [ ] subside
- [ ] substance
- [ ] successful
- [ ] sudden
- [ ] suffer
- [ ] sufficient
- [ ] sugar
- [ ] suggest
- [ ] suggestive
- [ ] sulphuric acid
- [ ] superficial

- [ ] support
- [ ] supply
- [ ] suppress
- [ ] suppuration
- [ ] suppurative
- [ ] surface
- [ ] surgeon
- [ ] surgery
- [ ] surgical
- [ ] surround
- [ ] survey
- [ ] survival
- [ ] survive
- [ ] susceptible
- [ ] suspect
- [ ] sustain
- [ ] sustained
- [ ] suture
- [ ] swab
- [ ] swallow
- [ ] sweat
- [ ] swell
- [ ] swelling
- [ ] sympathetic
- [ ] symptom
- [ ] synapse
- [ ] syncope
- [ ] syndrome
- [ ] synovial fluid
- [ ] synthesis
- [ ] synthetic
- [ ] syringe
- [ ] systemic
- [ ] systole
- [ ] systolic

T

☐ tablespoonful
☐ tactile
☐ technique
☐ temperature
☐ temporary
☐ tend
☐ tender
☐ tenderness
☐ tendon
☐ tension
☐ term
☐ test
☐ testis
☐ tetanus
☐ thalassaemia, thalassemia
☐ theatre, theater
☐ therapeutic
☐ therapist
☐ therapy
☐ thermometer
☐ thiamin(e)
☐ thick
☐ thigh
☐ thin
☐ thirst
☐ thorax
☐ thrill
☐ thrive
☐ throat

☐ thrombocytopenia
☐ thrombphlebitis
☐ thrombosis
☐ thymus
☐ thyroid
☐ thyroiditis
☐ thyrotoxicosis
☐ tibia
☐ tight
☐ time
☐ tincture
☐ tip
☐ tiredness
☐ tissue
☐ titre, titer
☐ toe
☐ tolerance
☐ tongue
☐ tone
☐ tonic
☐ tonsil
☐ tooth
☐ touch
☐ tourniquet
☐ toxic
☐ toxicity
☐ trace
☐ trachea
☐ tracing

☐ tract
☐ traction
☐ transfer
☐ transfusion
☐ translucent
☐ transmit
☐ transverse
☐ trauma
☐ treatment
☐ trial
☐ triceps
☐ tricuspid
☐ tricycle
☐ trigeminal
☐ trimester
☐ trolley
☐ trouble
☐ trunk
☐ tubercle
☐ tuberculosis
☐ tubule
☐ tumour, tumor
☐ turbid
☐ twins
☐ type
☐ typhoid fever
☐ typhus
☐ typical

U

☐ ulcer
☐ ulceration
☐ ulcerative colitis
☐ unbearable
☐ uncomplicated

☐ unconscious
☐ undergo
☐ underlying
☐ undernourished
☐ undertake

☐ undigested
☐ unfavourable, unfavorable
☐ uniform
☐ unit
☐ unknown

- ☐ unlikely
- ☐ unpleasant
- ☐ unsterile
- ☐ unusual
- ☐ upper

- ☐ uptake
- ☐ uraemia, uremia
- ☐ urea
- ☐ ureter
- ☐ ureteric

- ☐ urethra
- ☐ urgent
- ☐ urinary
- ☐ urine

V

- ☐ vaccinate
- ☐ vaccine
- ☐ vagina
- ☐ vaginal
- ☐ vague
- ☐ vagus
- ☐ valve
- ☐ valvular
- ☐ varices
- ☐ varicosity
- ☐ variety
- ☐ various
- ☐ vascular
- ☐ vasopressin

- ☐ vegetative
- ☐ vein
- ☐ vena cava
- ☐ ventilation
- ☐ ventricle
- ☐ ventricular
- ☐ vertebrae
- ☐ vertigo
- ☐ vessel
- ☐ via
- ☐ viable
- ☐ victim
- ☐ viral
- ☐ virulent

- ☐ virus
- ☐ viscera
- ☐ viscous
- ☐ vision
- ☐ visual
- ☐ vital
- ☐ vitreous
- ☐ voice
- ☐ volume
- ☐ vomit
- ☐ voyeurism
- ☐ vulva

W

- ☐ waist
- ☐ walk
- ☐ ward
- ☐ wash
- ☐ wasting
- ☐ water
- ☐ wave
- ☐ weak

- ☐ weakness
- ☐ weaning
- ☐ weigh
- ☐ weight
- ☐ well
- ☐ wheel stretcher
- ☐ white
- ☐ whole

- ☐ whooping cough
- ☐ wide
- ☐ widespread
- ☐ withdrawal
- ☐ work
- ☐ worms
- ☐ wound
- ☐ wrist

X

- ☐ xiphoid
- ☐ X-ray

Y

- ☐ year
- ☐ yellow fever
- ☐ yield
- ☐ young

Z

- ☐ zero
- ☐ zimmer

Medical Abbreviations

Abbreviations are used widely in medicine both in writing and in speech, but they *change rapidly.* Like much of language itself, abbreviations are subject to fashion. What is in use today might not be so common tomorrow. Abbreviations also differ from country to country and even perhaps from hospital to hospital. However, below is a selection of abbreviations you may meet in medical speech or writing. Many of these abbreviations, such as AIDS (acquired immune deficiency syndrome), CAT scan (computer-assisted tomography), DNA (deoxyribonucleic acid), or MS (Multiple scerosis), are universally understood and are often used without explanation. Modern writers tend not to use periods after letters. This is the convention adopted here.

A:	absorbance (in spectrophoto-metry)
	adrenaline
	adult
	allergy
	anesthetic
	argon (chemical symbol)
a:	acid
	anterior
	artery
A^2:	second aortic sound
AA:	Alcoholics Anonymous
AAA:	abdominal aortic aneurysm
	acute anxiety attack
AAE:	acute, allergic encephalitis
AAS:	aortic arch syndrome
	anthrax antiserum
AB:	abortion
	apex beat
ab:	antigen-binding capacity
abd:	abdomen
abdms (m) (t) (o):	abdomen without masses, tenderness, organo-megaly (US)
Abn:	abnormal
AC:	acetylcholine

	adrenal cortex
	air conduction
	alternating current
	anodal closure
	anti-inflammatory corticoid
ac:	before meals (Latin *ante cibum*)
	acute
ACD:	absolute cardiac dullness
AC-DC:	bisexual (homosexual and heterosexual)
ACE:	adrenal-cortical extract
	alcohol-chloroform-ether (mixture)
ACH:	arm, chest, height
ACH index:	arm girth, chest depth, hip width
act:	active
ACT:	anticoagulant therapy
ACTH:	adrenocorticotrophic hormone
AD:	antigenic determinant
	right ear (Latin *auris dextra*)
	drug addict
ADH:	antidiuretic hormone (vaso-pressin)
adm:	admission (to hospital)

152

Admin: administration
ADP: adenosine diphosphate
ADT: a placebo (any desired thing)
alternate day treatment
aet: age (Latin *aetas*)
aetiol. aetiology (UK)
AF: acid-fast
albumin free
amniotic fluid
atrial fibrillation (*also* A Fib)
AFB: acid-fast bacillus
AFP: alpha-fetoprotein
AG: antiglobulin
A/G: albumin/globulin (ratio)
Ag: antigen
AHA: Area Health Authority (UK)
AI: aortic incompetence
aortic insufficiency
artificial insemination
AID: acute infectious disease
autoimmune disease
AIDS: acquired immune deficiency
syndrome
AJ: ankle jerk
A.M.: morning (Latin *ante meridiem*)
AMA: American Medical Association
Amb: ambulance
AMI: acute myocardial
infarction
amp: ampere
ampoule
AN: antenatal
anal: analgesic
analysis
anesth: anesthesia, anesthetic
ang: angiogram
ANS: autonomic nervous system
anthropom: anthropometry
ant jentac: before breakfast (Latin *ante
jentaculum*)
AP: anteroposterior
aortic pressure
appendectomy
before dinner (Latin *ante
prandium*)
APH: antepartum hemorrhage
anterior pituitary hormone
appar: apparatus
apparent
approx: approximately (*also* appr)
APT: alum-precipitated toxoid
AQ: achievement or accomplishment
quotient
aq: water (Latin *aqua*)

AR: alarm reaction
analytical reagent
apical-radial pulse
ARM: artificial rupture of membranes
art: artery
artic. articulation
AS: alimentary system
ankylosing spondylitis
anxiety state
aortic stenosis
left ear (Latin *auris sinistra*)
As: astigmatism
ASAP: as soon as possible
ASCVD: arteriosclerotic cardiovascular
disease
ASD: atrial septal defect
ASHD: arteriosclerotic heart disease
(US)
ASO: antistreptolysin–O
ASR: aldosterone secretion rate
AST: antisyphilitic treatment
Ast: astigmatism
AT: adjunctive therapy
air temperature
at fib: atrial fibrillation
Athsc: atherosclerosis
atr: atrophy
ATS: antitetanus serum
anxiety tension state
aur fib: auricular fibrillation
aux: auxiliary
AV: aortic valve
atrioventricular
auriculoventricular
AVC: atrioventricular canal
A&W: alive and well
ax: axilla
axis
AZT: Aschheim-Zondek test (for
pregnancy)
azathioprine
B: bacillus
barometic
bicuspid
brother
buccal
b: born
BA: blood agar
bronchial asthma
buccoaxial
Ba: barium
BaE: barium enema
BaM: barium meal

BAP: blood-agar plate
brachial artery pressure
BB: bed bath
blood bank
breast biopsy
BBA: born before arrival
BBB: blood-brain barrier
BBT: basal body temperature
BC: bone conduction
buccocervical
BCG: Bacille Calmette-Guèrin
(vaccine)
BCG test: bicolor guaiac test
BD: bile duct
borderline duct
bd: twice a day (Latin *bis die*)
BDE: bile duct examination
BE: bile-esculin (test)
broncho-esophagology
BF: bentonite flocculation (test)
bouillon filtrate (tuberculin)
breast fed
BH: bill of health
brain hormone
BHIB: beef heart infusion broth
BI: bone injury
BID: brought in dead
bid: twice a day (Latin *bis in die*)
BIL: bilirubin (test)
bin: twice a night (Latin *bis in noctus*)
BIP: bacterial intravenous protein
biparietal diameter (of skull)
BIPP: bismuth iodoform paraffin paste
bkf: breakfast
BL: Burkitt's lymphoma
BlC: blood culture
BlS: blood sugar (*Also* BS)
BlT: blood type
BM: basal metabolism
bowel movement
BMA: British Medical Assocation
BNO: bowels not opened
BO: body odor
bowels open
BOA: born on arrival
bol: a large pill
BP: bed pan
birthplace
blood pressure
BPC: British Pharmaceutical Codex
BPD: biparietal diameter
BPH: benign prostatic hypertrophy
BR: bed rest

Br: bronchitis
brown
Brucella
Bronch: bronchoscopic
bronchoscopist
bronchoscopy
BS: blood sugar
breath sounds
BSA: body surface area
bovine serum albumin
BSp: bronchospasm
BSR: blood sedimentation rate
BST: blood serological test
BT: body temperature
BTB: breakthrough bleeding
BUN: blood urea nitrogen
BW: birth weight (*Also* B.Wt)
body water
body weight
BX: biopsy

C: carbon
cathode
centigrade (temperature scale)
certified
cervical
cocaine
control (group in/on experiment)
cortex
cytochrome
c: capacity
about (Latin *circa*)
with (Latin *cum*)
curie
C¹: complement (bacteriology)
C1, C2, C3: cytochromes 1, 2, and 3
C1, C14, C13: intermediate certificates for
1, 14, 13 weeks
C1 to C9: components of complement
CA: cardiac arrest
chronological age
cold agglutination (test)
coronary artery
Ca: calcium
carcinoma (*Also* CA)
cathode
CAAT: computer-assisted axial
tomography
CACX: cancer of the cervix
CAD: coronary artery disease
Capt: head presentation
CAT: coaxial or computed axial
tomography
CBC: complete blood count (US)

CC:	chest clinic
	critical condition
	current complaints
cc:	cubic centimeter
CCA:	cephalin cholesterol antigen
	chick cell agglutination (unit)
CCF:	congestive heart failure (UK)
CD:	casualty department
Cd:	cadmium
C&DB:	cough and deep breath
CDT:	carbon dioxide therapy
CE:	cardiac enlargement
	chloroform and ether mixture
	(*Also* C-E mixture)
	contractile element (of skeletal
	muscle)
	cytopathic effect
CEM:	conventional transmission
	electron microscope
cen:	centimeter (*Also* cm)
	central (*Also* cent)
cent:	centromere
CEO:	chick embryo origin
CEP:	countercurrent electrophoresis
cert:	certificate
	certified
cerv:	cervical
	cervix
CES:	central excitatory state
CF:	cancer-free
	cardiac failure
	colicin factor
	complement fixation
	counting fingers
	cystic fibrosis
CFT:	complement-fixation test
CG:	choking gas (phosgene)
	control group
cg:	centigram
	center of gravity
Cgh:	cough
cgm:	centigram (*Also* cg)
CGN:	chronic glomerulonephritis
CGP:	chorionic growth hormone –
	prolactin
	circulating granulocyte pool
CGS:	catgut suture
CH:	Christchurch chromosome
	crown – heel (length of fetus)
C&H:	cocaine and heroin
ch:	chest
	child
	choline
CHB:	complete heart block

CHD:	Chediak-Higashi disease
	coronary heart disease
ChE:	cholinesterase
chem:	chemistry
	chemical
CHF:	chronic heart failure
	congestive heart failure (US)
chg:	change
Chl:	chloroform
Chlb:	chlorobutonol
Chlor:	chloramphenicol
Chpx:	chickenpox
chr:	chronic
ChrCF:	chronic cardiac failure
CI:	cardiac index
	chemotherapeutic index
	color index
	contamination index
	coronary insufficiency
Ci:	curie
CIC:	cardioinhibitor center
CICU:	coronary intensive care unit
circ:	circuit
	circulation
	circulatory
	circumcised
	circumcision
CIS:	central inhibitory state
cit:	citrate
CL:	cholesterol-lecithin (test)
cm:	centimeter
CNS:	central nervous system
CO:	carbon monoxide
	cardiac output
	casualty officer (UK)
	centric occlusion
C/O:	check out
	complains of
CO_2:	carbon dioxide
COAD:	chronic obstructive airway
	disease (UK)
COC:	cathodal opening contraction
	combination (type) oral contra-
	ceptive
COD:	cause of death
cod:	codeine
coeff:	coefficient
COGTT:	cortisone (primed) oral glucose
	tolerance test
COH:	carbohydrate
COHb:	carboxyhemoglobin
C of H:	circumference of head
col:	colony (bacteriology)
	strain (Latin *cola*)

COLD: chronic obstructive lung disease
comp: complaint
complemented
composition
compd: compound
conj: conjunctiva
CONS: consultant
consulting
contra: contraindicated
COOH: carboxyl group
coord: coordination
COP: change of plaster
COPD: chronic obstructive pulmonary disease (us)
COPE: chronic obstructive pulmonary emphysema
COPRO: coproporphyrin
CP: cerebral palsy
chemically pure
cleft palate
color perception
compound
constant pressure
C/P: cholesterol/phospholipid (ratio)
C & P: cystoscopy and pyelography
Cp: chickenpox (*Also* Chpx)
CPB: cardiopulmonary bypass
CPD: citrate-phosphate-dextrose
contagious pustular dermatitis
CPE: chronic pulmonary emphysema
cytopathogenic effect
CSF: cerebrospinal fluid (fever)
colony-stimulating factor
CSM: cerebrospinal meningitis
CSR: corrected sedimentation rate
cortisol secretion rate
CSS: chronic subclinical scurvy
CSSD: Central Sterile Supply Depot (uk)
CST: Convulsive Shock Therapy
CSU: catheter specimen of urine
CT: cellular therapy
cerebral thrombosis
cerebral tumor
clotting (coagulation) time
connective tissue
corneal transplant
coronary thrombosis
CTS: computerized topographic scanner
CV: cardiovascular
cell volume
cerebrovascular
cervical vertebra

color vision
concentrated volume
conversational voice
CVA: cardiovascular accident
cerebrovascular accident
CVP: cell volume profile
central venous pressure
CVR: cardiovascular-renal (disease)
cardiovascular-respiratory
CVS: cardiovascular surgery
cardiovascular system
CW: case work
Children's Ward
CWBTS: capillary whole blood true sugar
CWS: cold water soluble
cwt: hundredweight
Cx: cervix
convex
CXR: chest X-ray
cyl: cylinder
CYS: cytoscopy
Cz: coryza
cytol: cytological
cytology
cyt sys: cytochrome system

D: give (Latin *da*)
dermatologist
dermatology
deviation
diagnosis
died
dispensing patient
dose (Latin *dosis*)
dull
dorsal
duration
divorced
d: density
died
dose
right (Latin *dexter*)
D/-: daily total in divided doses
DA: degenerative arthritis
delayed action (with reference to drugs)
dental anesthetic
developmental age
D/A: discharge and advise
D&C: dilation and curettage
DAD: dispense as directed
DAH: disordered action of the heart
DAO: duly authorized officer
DAP: diaminopimelic acid

	direct latex agglutination
	pregnancy (test)
DAT:	delayed action tablet
	diet as tolerated
	differential agglutination titer
DBP:	diastolic blood pressure
DBW:	desirable body weight
DC:	direct current
	distocervical
	donor cells (corpuscles)
DCN:	delayed conditioned necrosis
DCR:	dacryocystorhinostomy
	direct cortical response
DD:	dangerous drugs
	definitely dull
	differential diagnosis
	double diffusion (test)
	dry dressing
DDA:	Dangerous Drugs Act (UK)
D&D:	drunk and disorderly
D&E:	dilation and evacuation
dec:	pour off (Latin *deconta*)
	decrease
decub:	lying down (Latin *decubitus*)
DED:	date of expected delivery
	delayed erythema dose
Δ:	diagnosis
deriv:	derived from
Derm:	dermatological
	dermatology
DHR:	delayed hypersensitivity reaction
DI:	deterioration index
	diabetes insipid
diab:	diabetic
diag:	diagnosis (Also Δ)
	diagram
dias:	diastolic
diath:	diathermy
DIC:	drunk in charge
diff diag:	differential diagnosis
dil:	diluted (Also *dilut*)
diph:	diphtheria
d in p aeq:	divide into equal parts (Latin
	dividetur in partes aequales)
diph-tox AP:	diphtheria toxoid (alum pre-
	cipitated)
disloc:	dislocation
disp:	dispense
DJD:	degenerative joint disease
dl:	deciliter
DLE:	disseminated lupus erythema-
	tosus
DLI:	distolinguoincisal
DM:	diabetes mellitus

	diastolic murmur
DN:	District Nurse (UK)
D/N:	dextrose/nitrogen (ratio)
DNA:	deoxyribonucleic acid
	did not attend
DNC:	did not come
DNS:	deflected nasal septum
	did not suit
	dinoyl sebacate
DO:	diamine oxidase
DOA:	dead on arrival
DOB:	date of birth
dos:	dosage
DOPA (or DA): dopamine
DP:	deep pulse
	dementia precox
	diffusion pressure
	displaced person
	donor's plasma
DP/Vac: diphtheria pertussis prophylactic
	vaccine
DPT:	diphtheria, pertussis, tetanus
	(vaccine)
Dr:	Doctor
dr:	dorsal root (of spinal nerves)
	dressing
DRO:	Disablement Resettlement
	Officer (UK)
DRF:	daily replacement factor (of
	lymphocytes)
DS:	disseminated sclerosis
	double strength
	Down's syndrome
D/S:	dextrose/saline (ratio)
DSD:	dry sterile dressing
D.Sph:	diopter spherical
DST:	desensitization test
	dexamethasone suppression test
DT:	delirium tremens
	diptheria-tetanus [toxoid]
	dispensing tablet
	distance test
D/T:	deaths/total (ratio)
DT/VAC: diphtheria-tetanus vaccine
DTN:	diphtheria toxin, normal
DTP:	diphtheria, tetanus, pertussis
	(vaccine)
	distal tingling on percussion
DU:	duodenal ulcer
duod:	duodenum
dup:	duplicate
DV:	dilute volume
	distemper virus
	domiciliary visit

D&V:	diarrhea and vomiting
DVA:	duration of voluntary apnea (test)
DVT:	deep venous thrombosis
DW:	distilled water
D/w:	dextrose (5%) in water
Dx:	diagnosis
DXM:	dexamethasone (test for adrenocortical function)
DXR:	deep X-ray
DXRT:	deep X-ray therapy
DYSM:	dysmenorrhea
DZ:	dizygotic
E:	electrode potential
	electrolytes
	enzyme
	Escherichia (bacteriology)
	evening
	eye
e:	electron
EA:	erythrocyte antibody
EAA:	essential amino acid
EAC:	erythrocyte, antibody, complement
	external auditory canal
EACD:	eczematous allergic contact dermatitis
EAE:	experimental allergic encephalomyelitis
EAHF:	eczema, asthma, and hay fever
EaR:	reaction of degeneration (German *Entartungs-Reaktion*)
EB:	elementary body
	Epstein-Barr (virus)
EBS:	electric brain stimulation
	Emergency Bed Service
E-C:	ether-chloroform mixture
EC:	enteric coated (with reference to tablets)
	entering complaint
	extracellular
E/C:	estrogen/creatanine (ratio)
ECF:	extracellular fluid
ECG:	electrocardiogram
ECHO:	echoencephalogram
ECS:	electroconvulsive shock
ECT:	electroconvulsive therapy
ECV:	extracellular volume
ED:	effective dose
	erythema dose
Ed:	editor
ed:	edition
EDC:	expected date of confinement

EDD:	enzyme-digested delta (endotoxin)
	expected date of delivery
EDM:	early diastolic murmur
EDP:	end-diastolic pressure
EDR:	effective direct radiation
	electrodermal response
EE:	equine encephalitis
	eye and ear
E-E:	erythematous-edematous (reaction) (us)
EEG:	electroencephalogram
	electroencephalograph
EENT:	eye, ear, nose, and throat
EF:	edema factor (us)
	extrinsic factor
EFA:	essential fatty acid
EGF:	epidermal growth factor
EH:	enlarged heart
EHBF:	extrahepatic blood flow
EKG:	electrocardiogram (us)
E&M:	endocrine and metabolic
Emb:	embryology
EMC:	encephalomyocarditis
EMF:	electromotive force
	endomyocardial fibrosis
	erythrocyte maturation factor
EMG:	electromyogram
	electromyograph
EMS:	early morning specimen
EN:	erythema nodosum
Endocrin:	endocrinology
ENT:	ear, nose, and throat
EOM:	extraocular movement
EOS:	eosinophil(s)
EOU:	epidemic observation unit
EP:	ectopic pregnancy
	extreme pressure
	electrophoresis
ERIA:	electroradioimmunoassay
ERPF:	effective renal plasma flow
ES:	emergency service
	enema saponis
ESF:	erythropoietic stimulating factor
ESN:	educationally subnormal
esoph:	esophagus (us)
esp:	especially
ESR:	erythrocyte sedimentation rate
ETT:	exercise tolerance test
ETU:	emergency treatment unit
EUA:	examination under anesthetic
EV:	evoked response
	extravascular
EW:	emergency ward

EWL:	evaporative water loss	FHH:	fetal heart heard
exp:	expected	FHNH:	fetal heart not heard
	experiment (*Also* expt)	FHS:	fetal heart sounds
expir:	expiration, expiratory	FHT:	fetal heart tone
EXTREM: external radiation dose		fib:	fibrositis
ext fl:	fluid extract	fibrill:	fibrillation
ext rot:	external rotation	fig:	figuratively
Ez:	eczema		figure
		filt:	filter
F:	facies	FIN:	fine intestinal needle
	Fahrenheit (temperature scale)	F-insul:	fibrous insulin
	family	fl:	femtoliter
	father		focal length
	fasting (test)	FM:	flavin mononucleotide
	female		fusobacteria microorganism
	fluorine		make a mixture (Latin *fiat*
	french (catheter size)		*mistura*)
	full (with reference to diet)	FMD:	foot and mouth disease
f:	fluid	FME:	full mouth extraction
	focal	FMF:	familial Mediterranean fever
	frequency		fetal movement felt
FA:	fatty acid	FMN:	flavin mononucleotide
	febrile antigens	FMP:	first menstrual period
	filterable agent	FMS:	fat-mobilizing substance
	fortified aqueous (solution)	FMX:	full mouth X-ray (dentistry)
	Freund's adjuvout	FP:	family planning
FAA sol:	formalin, acetic, alcohol solution		food poisoning
	(a fixative)		flavoprotein
FAB:	antigen-binding fragments	FPC:	family planning clinic
	functional arm brace		(UK)
Fb:	finger breadth		fish protein concentrate
FB:	foreign body	FPM:	filter paper microscopic test
FBC:	full blood count	F&R:	force and rhythm (of pulse)
FBCOD: foreign body of the cornea,		FR:	failure rate (contraception)
	right eye (Latin *oculus dexter*)		fixed rate
FBCOS: foreign body of the cornea,			flocculation reaction
	left eye (Latin *oculus sinister*)	FRF:	follicle-stimulating hormone-
FBS:	fasting blood sugar		releasing factor
	fetal bovine serum	frict:	friction
FCT:	food composition table	Fried test: Friedman test (for pregnancy)
FD:	fatal dose	FS:	frozen section
	focal distance		full and soft (diet)
	forceps delivery	FSH:	follicle-stimulating hormone
	freeze-dried	FSU:	family service unit
fdg:	feeding	FT:	follow through (after BaM)
FDIU:	fetal death *in utero*		formal toxoid
FDNB:	fluorodinitrobenzene		free thyroxine
FDP:	fibrin degradation product		full term
	fructose diphosphate	FTAT:	fluorescent treponemal antibody
FE:	fetal erythroblastosis		test
Fe:	iron (Latin *ferrum*)	FTBD:	fit to be detained
FECG:	fetal electrocardiogram		full term born dead
FH:	family history	FTM:	fractional test meal
	fetal heart	FTND:	full term normal delivery

FU:	fecal urobilinogen		GPB:	glossopharyngeal breathing
	fluorouracil		GPC:	general physical condition
	fractional urinalysis		GPI:	general paralysis of the insane
FUB:	functional uterine bleeding		GPS:	guinea pig serum
FUO:	fever of unknown origin		GPT:	glutamic pyruvic transaminase
FVC:	forced vital capacity		Gp Th:	group therapy
FW:	forced whisper		GR:	gamma ray
Fx:	fracture			gastric resection
				glutathione reductase
G:	gas		gr:	gamma roentgen
	gastrin			gravity
	gauge		GRAE:	generally regarded as effective
	globulin		gran:	granulated (Latin *granulatus*)
	glucose		grav:	gravid (pregnant)
	gram(s)		GRF:	growth hormone – releasing
g:	gender			factor
	gram(s)		GS:	general surgery
Γ :	(Greek letter gamma, third letter			glomerular sclerosis
	of Gk. alphabet)		g/s:	gallons per second
	heavy chain of immunogamma-		GSA:	general somatic afferent (nerve)
	globulin		GSC:	gravity settling culture (plate)
GA:	gastric analysis		GSD:	glycogen storage disease
	general anesthetic		GSR:	galvanic skin response
	gingivoaxial			generalized Schwartzman
	glucuronic acid			reaction
G and A:	gas and air		GT:	genetic therapy
GALT:	gut-associated lymphoid tissue			glucose tolerance
GAS:	general adaptation syndrome			group therapy
	general arteriosclerosis		GTN:	glyceryl trinitrate
	gastroenterology		GTT:	glucose tolerance test
GB:	gall bladder		g/t:	granulation time
	Guillain-Barré (syndrome)			granulation tissue
GBS:	gall bladder series		GU:	gastric ulcer
	glycerine buffered saline			genito-urinary
GC:	gas chromatography			glycogenic unit
	general condition			gonococcal urethritis
	gonococcal infection (gonor-			gravitational ulcer
	rhea)		GUS:	genito-urinary system
GCFT:	gonococcal complement		GV:	gentian violet
	fixation test		GVA:	general visceral afferent (nerve)
GEF:	gonadotrophin enhancing factor		GVE:	general visceral efferent (nerve)
genet:	genetics		GVH:	graft versus host (reaction)
genit:	genitalia		Gvty:	gingivectomy
gen proc:	general procedure		GW:	glycerine in water
GET:	gastric emptying time		GYN:	gynecologist
GI:	gastrointestinal			gynecology
	globin insulin			
	growth inhibiting		H:	flagella (bacteriology)
GIl:	gastrointestinal infection			heroin
GLA:	gingivolinguoaxial			Holzknecht unit
GOT:	glutamic oxalacetic transaminase			hospital
GP:	general paralysis			hydrogen
	general practitioner			hypodermic
	Gram – positive		h:	height
	guinea pig			horizontal

HA:	hemoadsorption (test)
	hemagglutination
	hemolytic anemia
	hepatitis-associated (virus)
HAA:	hemolytic anemia antigen
	hepatitis-associated antigen
HAc:	acetic acid
hem:	hemolysis (with reference to blood fragility test)
hemat:	hematocrit
	hematology
hemorrh:	hemorrhage
HAS:	highest asymptomatic (dose)
	hypertensive arteriosclerotic
H&ASHD:	hypertension and arteriosclerotic heart disease
HAV:	hepatitis A virus
HB:	heart block
	hepatitis B
Hb:	hemoglobin
HBAg:	hepatitis B antigen
HBF:	hepatic blood flow
HbF:	fetal hemoglobin
HBP:	high blood pressure
HbP:	primitive (fetal) hemoglobin
HbS:	sickle-cell hemoglobin
HC:	handicapped
	head circumference
	home care
	hydrocarbon
	hydrocortisone
HCS:	hospital car service
Hct:	hematocrit
HCVD:	hypertensive cardiovascular disease
HD:	hemolysing dose
	heart disease
	hearing distance
	high density
	Hodgkin's disease
HDL:	high density lipoprotein
HDN:	hemolytic disease of the newborn
HDU:	hemodialysis unit
HE:	human enteric
HEAT:	human erythrocyte agglutination test
hemat:	hematology
hemi:	hemiparalysis
	hemiplegia
hern:	hernia, herniated
HF:	Hageman factor (in blood plasma)
	hay fever
	heart failure

HFC:	hard filled capsules
HofF:	height of fundus
HG:	human gonadotrophin
hgb:	hemoglobin
HH:	hard of hearing
	Henderson and Haggard (inhaler)
	home help
HHb:	reduced hemoglobin
HHD:	hypertensive heart disease
HI:	hemoagglutination inhibition
	hospital insurance
HID:	headache, insomnia, depression (syndrome)
HIG:	human immunoglobulin
Hint:	Hinton (flocculation test for syphilis)
HIP:	health insurance plan
	hydrostatic indifference point
hist:	history
histol:	histology
HM:	hand movements
	herd movements
HMD:	hyaline membrane disease
HME:	heat, massage, exercise
HN:	head nurse
HO:	house officer (UK)
HOCM:	hypertrophic obstructive cardiomyopathy
Homeop:	homeopathy
homo:	homosexual
HOS:	human
HP:	handicapped person
	highly purified
	house physician (UK)
	human prolactin
	hyperphoria
H&P:	hypertension and proteinuria
	history and physical (examination)
HPL:	human parotid lysozyme
	human placental lactogen
HPN:	hypertension
HPS:	high protein supplement
HR:	heart rate
hr:	hour
HRE:	high resolution electrocardiography
HS:	Hartman's solution
	heart sounds
	homologous serum
	house supervisor
	house surgeon
H&S:	hysterectomy and sterilization
HSA:	human serum albumin

HSD:	hydroxysteroid dehydrogenase	Ig:	immunoglobulin
HSG:	herpes simplex genitalis	IGH:	immunoreactive growth hormone
HSL:	herpes simplex labialis	IH:	infectious hepatitis
HSV:	herpes simplex virus		inhibiting hormone
5-HT:	5-hydroxytryptamine (seroto-		iron hematoxylin
	nin)	IHD:	ischemic heart disease
Hx:	history	IHSS:	idiopathic hypertrophic
	hypoxanthine		subaortic stenosis
Hydro:	hydrotherapy	IJP:	inhibitory junction potential
HYP:	hypnosis	ILM:	insulin-like material
Hypo:	hypodermic injection	Ilo:	iodine solution
hys:	hysteria	IM:	Index Medicus
			infectious mononucleosis
I:	index		internal medicine
	inhibitor		intramuscular
	internist (us)	immat:	immature
	iodine	Immunol:	immunology
i:	incisor (deciduous)	Impr:	improved
	optically inactive	IN:	icterus neonatorum
IA:	intra-arterial		intranasal
	intra-atrial		initial dose
IAS:	intra-amniotic saline (infusion)	ing:	inguinal
IASD:	interatrial septal defect	inj:	inject(ion)
IAT:	iodine azide test		injury
IB:	immune body	in situ:	in natural or normal position
	infectious bronchitis	intern:	internal
IBW:	ideal body weight	INTEST:	intestinal
IC:	intensive care	INTOX:	intoxicated
	intercostal		intoxication
	intracardiac	*in utero*:	within the uterus
	intracutaneous (injection)	*in vitro*:	within glass
ICD:	international classification of		within a test tube
	diseases	*in vivo*:	within a living body
ICF:	indirect centrifugal flotation	I & O:	intake and output
	intensive care facility	IOFB:	intraocular foreign body
	intracellular fluid	IOP:	intraocular pressure
ICM:	intercostal margin	IP:	icterus precox
ICS:	intercostal space		incisoproximal
ICT:	icterus		incubation period
	inflammation of connective tissue		inpatient
	insulin coma therapy		insurance patient
ICU:	intensive care unit		interphalangeal
ID:	infectious disease	IPV:	inactivated poliomyelitis vaccine
	infective dose		infectious pustular vaginitis
	intradermal(ly)	IQ:	intelligence quotient
I&D:	incision and drainage	IR:	inferior rectus (muscle)
IEA:	intravascular erythrocyte		infrared
	aggregation	I-R:	Ito-Reenstierna (reaction)
IEC:	injection electrode catheter	IRM:	innate releasing mechanism
	intra-epithelial carcinoma	IRRG:	irrigated
IF:	immunofluorescence (test)		irrigation
	interstitial fluid	IRL:	infrared light
	intrinsic factor	IRU:	industrial rehabilitation unit
If nec:	if necessary	ISF:	interstitial fluid

isom:	isometric
ISQ:	unchanged (Latin *in status quo*)
IST:	insulin shock therapy
i-sub:	inhibitor substance
IT:	inhalation therapy
	intrathoracic
	intubercular
ITR:	intratracheal
ITT:	insulin tolerance test
IU:	immunizing unit
	international unit
	intrauterine
IUD:	intrauterine device
IV:	interventricular
	intervertebral
	intravenous
	intraventricular
iv:	iodine value
IVC:	inferior vena cava
	intravenous cholangiogram
IVCD:	intraventricular conduction defect
IVF:	intravascular fluid
IVP:	intravenous pyleogram
IVSD:	intravenous septal defect
IVT:	intravenous transfusion
IVU:	intravenous urogram
IYS:	inverted Y-suspensor
IZS:	insulin zinc suspension
J:	joint
	Jaeger type
jaund:	jaundice
jct:	junction
JJ:	jaw jerk
Jour:	journal
JV:	jugular vein
JVD:	jugular venous distension (US)
JVP:	jugular vein pulse
	jugular venous pressure (UK)
K:	absolute zero
	electrostatic capacity
	Kelvin (temperature scale)
k:	constant
	kilo
KA:	alkaline phosphatase
	ketoacidosis
KB:	ketone bodies
KE:	Kendall's compound E (cortisone)
	kinetic energy
Kf:	symbol for flocculation speed in antigen-antibody reaction
KI:	Krönig's isthmus
	potassium iodide
KJ:	knee jerk
Kl bac:	Klebs-Loeffler bacillus (diphtheria bacillus)
KP:	keratitis punctata
KS:	ketosteroid
KST:	kathodal (cathodal) closing tetanus
KUB:	kidney, ureter, and bladder
	kidney and upper bladder
kw:	kilowatt
L:	left
	lethal
	liter
l:	left
	levorotatory
	long
LA:	left angle
	left atrium
	local anesthesia
	local authority
	long-acting (drug)
L&A:	light and accommodation (with reference to pupil reaction)
lab:	laboratory
lab proc:	laboratory procedure
LaC:	labiocervical
LAD:	lactic acid dehydrogenase
	left axis deviation
lam:	laminectomy
lap:	laporoscopy
	laporotomy
LAR:	laryngologist
	laryngology
LAS:	linear alkyl sulphonate
	local adaptation syndrome
lb:	pound (of weight) (Latin *libra*)
LATS:	long-acting thyroid stimulator
LBP:	lower back pain
	low blood pressure
LCA:	left coronary artery
LCCS:	low cervical cesarian section
LCFA:	long chain fatty acid
LD:	lactic dehydrogenase
	lethal dose
	living donor
	low density
LDA:	left dorsoanterior (position of fetus)
LDH:	lactic dehydrogenase
LDL:	low density lipoprotein
LDP:	left dorsoposterior (position of fetus)

Lect: lecturer
leg: legal(ly)
LE: left eye
            lupus erythematosus
LES: local excitatory state
            lower esophageal sphincter (us)
Lf: limit of flocculation
LFA: left frontoanterior (left mento-
            anterior) (position of fetus)
LFD: low fat diet
LFH: left femoral hernia
LFP: left frontoposterior (left mento-
            posterior) (position of fetus)
LFT: latex fixation test
LFTS: lung function tests
LH: left hand
            left hyperphoria
            lower half
LIF: left inguinal fossa
LIH: left inguinal hernia
LHRF: luteinizing hormone releasing
            factor
LLL: lower left lobe
LLQ: left lower quadrant
LMC: local medical committee
LMN: lower motor neuron
LMP: last menstrual period
            left mentoposterior (position of
            fetus)
            lumbar puncture
LO: linguo-occlusal
LOA: leave of absence
            left occipito-anterior (position of
            fetus)
LOP: leave on pass
            left occipito-posterior (position
            of fetus)
LOT: left occipito-transverse (position
            of fetus)
LP: laboratory procedure
            latent period
            lipoprotein
            low pressure
            lumbar puncture
LPF: leucocytosis-promoting factor
LPL: lipoprotein lipase
LR: laboratory report
            lateral rectus (muscle)
LRI: lower respiratory infection
LRF: liver residue factor
            luteinizing hormone releasing
            factor
LS: lateral suspensor
            liminal sensitivity
            lumbosacral

LSA: left sacro-anterior (position of
            fetus)
LSK: liver, spleen, kidneys
LSCS: lower segment cesarian section
LU: left upper
LUA: left upper arm
LUQ: left upper quadrant
LV: left ventricle
            live vaccine
            lumbar vertebra
LVA: left visual acuity
LVE: left ventricular enlargement
LVF: left ventricular failure
LVH: left ventricular hypertrophy
L&W: live and well
lymph: lymphocyte
lytes: electrolytes
LZM: lysozyme

M: male
            malignant
            married
            mature
            minimum
            molar
            morning
            mother
            motile (bacteria)
            myopia
m: meter
            minute
M1, M2, M3: slight, marked, and
            absolute dullness (auscultation)
M1:   mitral (first) sound
MA: menstrual age
            mental age
ma: milliampere
MABP: mean arterial blood pressure
MAF: minimum audible field
MAO: monoamine oxidase
MAOI: monoamine oxidase inhibitor
mass: massage
mast: mastoid
Mc: megacurie
            megacycle
mc: millicurie
MCB: membranous cytoplasmic body
McB: McBurney's (point)
MCCU: mobile coronary care unit
MCD: mean corpuscular diameter
mcg: microgram
MCH: mean corpuscular hemoglobin
MCHC: mean corpuscular hemoglobin
            concentration

MCL: midclavicular line
Mcps: megacycles per second
MCV: mean corpuscular volume
MD: manic depressive
    mean deviation
    mentally deficient
    mitral disease
    muscular dystrophy
MDF: myocardial depressant factor
MDH: malate dehydrogenase
MDM: mid-diastolic murmur
MDQ: minimum detectable quantity
MDR: minimum daily requirement
ME: maximum effort
    middle ear
meas: measurement
mech: mechanical
MED: median erythrocyte diameter
    medicine
    minimal effective dose
MEDLARS: Medical Literature Analysis
    and Retrieval System
MEDLINE: an on-line segment of
    MEDLARS
Med Tech: Medical Technician
MEM: minimum essential medium
MEP: mean effective pressure
    motor end-plate
Meth: methodrin
mEq: milliequivalent(s)
M/F: male/female (ratio)
MF: mycosis fungoides
MFT: muscle function test
Mg: magnesium
mg: milligram
MH: marital history
    menstrual history
    mental health
MHb: myohemoglobin
MHO: medical health officer
MI: mitral insufficiency
    metabolic index
    myocardial infarction
MICU: mobile intensive care unit
MID: minimal inhibiting dose
mid: middle
MIF: migration-inhibiting factor (for
    macrophages)
MIFR: maximal inspiratory flow rate
mil: military
min: mineral
    minimum
    minute
misc: miscarriage

miscellaneous
mit insuf: mitral insufficiency
MJ: marijuana
MK: monkey kidney
m-kg: meter-kilogram
mL: millilambert
ml: milliliter (1/1000 of a liter)
MLC: mixed leucocyte culture
MLT: median lethal time (radiation)
    medical laboratory technician
mm: millimeter
    muscles
MMR: mass miniature radiography
mm st: muscle strength
MMT: manual muscle test
MN: mononuclear (leucocyte)
    motor neuron
MO: medical officer (UK)
mo: month
MOH: medical officer of health (UK)
mol: molecule
mol wt: molecular weight
MOM: milk of magnesia
MOP: medical outpatient
Mon: Monday
MPN: most probable number
MPNI: Ministry of Pensions and
    National Insurance
MR: manual removal
    may repeat
    mentally retarded
MRA: medical record administrator
MRU: mass radiography unit
    minimal reproductive units
    (bacteriology)
MRV: mixed respiratory vaccine
MS: mass spectrometry
    mitral stenosis
    molar solution
    multiple sclerosis
    muscle strength
    musculoskeletal
Mss: manuscripts
MSSU: mid-stream specimen of urine
MSV: murine sarcoma virus
MSW: medical social worker (UK)
mμ: millimicron
MVP: mitral valve prolapse
MWO: mental welfare officer
My: myopia
MXR: mass X-ray
MZ: monozygotic
μ: micron
μg: microgram(s)

N:	nasal	NGF:	nerve growth factor
	negative	NGU:	nongonococcal urethritis
	nerve	NH:	nursing home
	Nonne (globulin test)	NI:	national insurance
n:	born (Latin *natus*)		not found
	nano (prefix)	NIC:	national insurance certificate
	neutron		(UK)
NA:	Narcotics Anonymous	NIL:	not in labor
	National Assistance	NK:	not known
	nicotinic acid	NM:	negro male
	Nomina Anatomica		neuromuscular
	noradrenaline		night and morning
	not applicable		nuclear medicine
NAA:	nicotinic acid amide	NMI:	no middle initial
	no apparent abnormalities	NMT:	neuromuscular tension
NAD:	no acute distress	NMU:	neuromuscular unit
	no appreciable disease	nn:	nerves
	nothing abnormal detected	NND:	neonatal death
Na$_e$:	exchangeable body sodium	nocte:	at night (Latin *nocte*)
NAG:	nonagglutinating	norm:	normal
NAH:	not at home	NP:	nasopharynx
NAI:	nonaccidental injury		near point
NAR:	nasal airway resistance		not palpable
NARC:	narcotic		not practiced
	narcotics officer		proper name (label with) (Latin
narco:	narcotics hospital		*nomen proprium*)
	narcotics officer	NPD:	Niemann-Pick's disease
Nat:	national	NPT:	normal pressure and temperature
NB:	note well, take notice (Latin *nota*	NPU:	not passed urine
	bene)	NR:	do not repeat (in prescriptions)
	newborn		neutral red (on indicator)
NBI:	no bone injury		no response
NBM:	nothing by mouth		normal range
NBTNF:	newborn, term, normal, female	NRS:	normal rabbit serum
NBTNM:	newborn, term, normal, male	NS:	nervous system
ND:	natural death		not seen
	neoplastic disease		neurosurgeon
	nervous disability		neurosurgery
	normal delivery	NSA:	no significant abnormality
	not diagnosed	nsa:	no salt added
	not done	NSAID:	nonsteroidal anti-inflammatory
NDA:	new drug application		drug
NE:	neurological examination	NSD:	no significant defect
	norepinephrine	nsg:	nursing
	not enlarged	NSPCC:	National Society for the Preven-
	not examined		tion of Cruelty to Children (UK)
neut:	neuter	NT:	nasotracheal
	neutral		neutralization test
NFTD:	normal full term delivery		no test
NFV:	no further visit	N&T:	nose and throat
NG:	nasogastric	NTP:	normal temperature and pressure
	new growth	NTR:	nutrition
	no good	nucl:	nucleus
ng:	nanogram (millimicrogram)	NV:	next visit

	nonvaccinated		OH:	occupational health
	nonvenereal			occupational history
N&V:	nausea and vomiting			outpatient hospital
Nv:	naked vision		OHC:	outer hair cells
NYD:	not yet diagnosed		OHD:	organic heart disease
Nyst:	nystagmus		OI:	opsonic index
				orgasmic impairment
O:	occlusal		OIH:	ovulation-inducing hormone
	eye (Latin *oculus*)		oint:	ointment
	old		OIT:	organic integrity test (psychiatry)
	opium		OJ:	orange juice
	oral(ly)		OK:	correct, approved, all right
	oxygen		OL:	left eye (Latin *oculus laevus*)
	without film (bacteria)		Ol:	oil (Latin *oleum*)
O_2:	both eyes		OM:	occupational medicine
	oxygen			osteomyelitis
O_2sat:	oxygen saturation			otitis media
OA:	occiput anterior		om:	every morning (Latin *omni mane*)
	old age		OM&S:	osteopathic medicine and surgery
	on admission		ON:	orthopaedic nurse (UK)
	osteoarthritis		OOB:	out of bed
OAF:	open air factor		OP:	occiput posterior
OAP:	old age pension(er) (UK)			operative procedure
OAS:	old age security			osmotic pressure
OB:	obstetrics			outpatient
ob:	he died, she died (Latin *obiit*)		op:	operation
OBS:	obstetrical service			opposite
	organic brain syndrome		o & p:	ova and parasites
obst:	obstruction		opg:	opening
OC:	occlusocervical		OPH:	ophthalmology
	office call		OPS:	outpatient service
	only child		orig:	original
	oral contraceptive		OR:	operating room (US)
occ:	occasional(ly)		ORS:	oral surgeon
	occlusion		ORT:	operating room technician
occTh:	occupational therapist		Ortho:	orthopedics (UK)
	occupational therapy		OS:	left eye (Latin *oculus sinister*)
OD:	occupational disease			Osgood Schlatter's (disease)
	right eye (Latin *oculus dexter*)			osteogenic sarcoma
	optical density		os:	bone (Latin *os*)
	out of date			mouth (Latin *oris*)
	overdose		OT:	occupational therapy
od:	daily (Latin *omni die*)			old tuberculin
ODA:	right occipito-anterior (position			orotracheal
	of fetus) (Latin *occipito-dextra*			otology
	anterior)			operating theatre (UK)
OE:	on examination		OTD:	organ tolerance dose
	otitis externa		OTO:	otology
oed:	oedema (UK)		ou:	both eyes together (Latin *oculi*
O&E:	observation and examination			*unitas*)
oesoph:	oesophagous (UK)		OV:	overventilation (hyperventilation)
OG:	obstetrics and gynecology		ov:	egg (Latin *ovum*)
	occlusogingival		OW:	out of wedlock
OGTT:	oral glucose tolerance test		oz:	ounce

P: pain
         patient
         percussion
         pharmacopeia
         poison
         plasma
         population
         prescribing
         private
         prolactin
         pulse
P_1:   first parental generation (in
         genetics)
P_2:   second pulmonic heart sound
PA: paralysis agitans
         pernicious anemia
         platelet adhesiveness
         postero-anterior
         prior to admission
         pulmonary artery
P_A: partial pressure in arterial blood
P&A: percussion and auscultation
PAC: premature atrial contraction
paed: paediatric (UK)
Pap: Pap smear (Papanicolaou)
Para: Formula meaning: P=number of
         pregnancies;
         a=number of abortions or
         miscarriages;
         ra=number of living children,
         e.g., Para 3+1=3 full term
         pregnancies, 1 abortion
parox: paroxysmal
PARU: postanesthetic recovery unit
PAT: paroxysmal atrial tachycardia
PB: phenobarbitone
         pressure breathing
PBI: protein bound iodine
PBX: phenylbutazone
pc: after food (Latin *post cibum*)
         percent
PCA: passive cutaneous anaphylaxis
PDA: pediatric allergy
         patent ductus arteriosus
Pen: penicillin
PE: Edinburgh Pharmacopeia
         physical examination
         pulmonary embolism
Pe: pressure on expiration
PED: pediatrics (US)
PERRLA: pupils equal, round, react to
         light and accommodation
PET: pre-eclamptic toxemia
petr: petroleum
PFU: plaque forming unit

PFV: physiological full value
PH: past history
         public health
pH: symbol for expression of
         hydrogen ion concentration
PHE: post heparin esterase
phial: bottle (Latin *phiala*)
PHK cells: postmortem human kidney
         cells
Phy: pharyngitis
         physician
PHLS: public health laboratory service
PHP: post-heparin phospholipase
         prepaid health plan
Phys Ed: physical education
physio: physiotherapist
         physiotherapy
Phys Med: physical medicine
PI: pressure of inspiration
         pulmonary insufficiency
PIC: postinflammatory corticoid
PICU: pulmonary intensive care unit
PID: pelvic inflammatory disease
         prolapsed invertebral disc
PL: perception of light
         phospholipid
         plastic surgeon
pl: place
         plasma
         plural
PM: passed motion
         petit mal
         physical medicine
         postmortem
         prostatic massage
         pulpomesial
PMA: papillary, marginal, attached
         (gingivae)
         progressive muscular atrophy
PMB: postmenopausal bleeding
PMD: progressive muscular dystrophy
PMI: point of maximal impulse (of
         heart on chest wall)
         previous medical illness
PMO: Principal Medical Officer
PMP: persistent mentoposterior
         (position of fetus)
         previous menstrual period
PMS: postmenopausal syndrome
         premenstrual syndrome
PMT: premenstrual tension
PN: percussion note
         peripheral nerve
         postnatal
         practical nurse

Pn:	pneumonia	PSW:	psychiatric social worker (UK)
PND:	paroxysmal nocturnal dyspnea	PT:	patient
	postnasal drip		physical training
PNF:	proprioceptive neuromuscular		pulmonary tuberculosis
	facilitation	PTA:	prior to admission
PNI:	peripheral nerve injury	PTAP.	purified diphtheria toxoid
	postnatal infection		precipitated by aluminium
PNO:	Principal Nursing Officer		phosphate
PNS:	parasympathetic nervous system	PTx:	parathyroidectomy
	peripheral nervous system	PU:	passed urine
Pnx:	pneumothorax		peptic ulcer
PO:	period of onset		per urethram
	postoperative	PuD:	pulmonary disease
PO₂:	pressure of oxygen	PUO:	pyrexia of unknown origin
po:	by mouth (Latin *per os*)	PV:	paraventricular (nucleus)
pois:	poison		per vaginam
polio:	poliomyelitis		pressure/volume
POMR:	problem oriented medical record	PVD:	peripheral vascular disease
POP:	plasma osmotic pressure		pulmonary vascular disease
	plaster of paris	PVT:	paroxysmal ventricular
pop:	popular		tachycardia
pos:	position	PX:	physical examination
	positive	Px:	past history
PP:	private patient		prognosis
	pulse pressure	Pyr:	pyridine
	pyrophosphate	PZI:	protamine zinc insulin
PPD:	progressive perceptive deafness		
	purified protein derivative	Q:	quantity
	(tuberculin)		quotient
PPH:	postpartum hemorrhage		volume of blood
PPS:	postpartum sterilization	q:	each, every (Latin quaque)
ppt:	precipitate	qds:	four times a day (Latin *quater die*
	prepared		*sumendum*)
PR:	*per rectum*	qid:	four times a day (Latin *quater in*
	pityriasis rosea		*die*)
	pregnancy rate	QNS:	quantity not sufficient
	pulse rate	qod:	every other day (Latin *quoque*
pr:	pair		*die*)
	per rectum	QRS:	segment of electrocardiograph
pract:	practical	QT:	Quick's Test (for pregnancy or
prn:	as required, whenever necessary		prothrombin)
	(Latin *pro re nata*)	qual:	quality
prem:	premature	quar:	quarterly
	premature infant	quot:	as often as necessary (Latin
prob:	probability		*quoties*)
	problem	quotid:	daily (Latin *quotidie*)
proc:	proceedings		
	procedure	R:	race
prod:	product		rectal
Prof:	professor		red
PROM:	premature rupture of membranes		resistance
PS:	per speculum		respiration
	plastic surgery		response
	pulmonary stenosis		right
P&S:	paracentesis and suction	Rₓ:	take treatment (Latin *recipe*)

r:	roentgen		rough, noncapsulated, avirulent
RA:	radioactive		(bacterial culture)
	repeat action	roent:	roentgenologist
	rheumatoid arthritis		roentgenology
	right atrium	ROA:	right occipital anterior
RAD:	right axis deviation	ROM:	range of movement
rad:	radiation	Rom:	Romberg
	radical	ROO:	Resident Obstetric Officer (UK)
RAT:	repeat action tablet	ROP:	right occipital posterior
RBC:	red blood cell count	Rpt:	repeat
	red blood corpuscle (cell)	Ror:	Rorschach (test)
RBD:	right border of dullness (heart	RS:	respiratory system
	percussion)		Reye's syndrome
RBS:	random blood sugar		Ringer's solution
RC:	red cell	RSO:	Resident Surgical Officer
	Red Cross	RSR:	regular sinus rhythm
	respiratory care	RST:	radiosensitivity testing
	Roman Catholic	RSV:	Rous sarcoma virus
RCA:	right coronary artery	RTA:	road traffic accident
RCD:	relative cardiac dullness		renal tube acidosis
Re:	response	RTC:	return to clinic
RD:	reaction of degeneration	RTF:	resistance transfer factor
	registered dietitian		respiratory tract fluid
	respiratory disease	rtl:	rectal
Rd:	reading	R test:	reductase test
RdA:	reading age	RTR:	red blood cell turnover rate
RDS:	respiratory distress syndrome	RU:	rat unit
RE:	rectal examination		Roentgen unit
	right eye	RUA:	right upper arm
resus:	resuscitation	RV:	right ventricle
Rh:	Rhesus factor		rubella vaccine
	rheumatism	RVA:	renal vascular resistance
RHA:	Regional Health Authority		right visual acuity
	(UK)	RVD:	relative vertebral density
RHD:	relative hepatic dullness	RVH:	right ventricular hypertrophy
	rheumatic heart disease	RVLG:	right ventrolateral gluteal (site of
rheu fev:	rheumatic fever		injection)
RHS:	right hand side	RVO:	relaxed vaginal outlet
RI:	radiation intensity	RVS:	relative value scale
	respiratory infection		reported visual sensation
RIA:	radioimmunoassay	Rx:	prescription
RIF:	right iliac fossa		take treatment or therapy (Latin
RIGH:	rabies immune globulin, human		*recipe*)
RIH:	right inguinal hernia		
RL:	right lower	S:	sacral
	Ringer lactate		schedule
RLC:	residual lung capacity		sensitive
RLL:	right lower lobe		single dose
RM:	radical mastectomy		soluble
	range of movement		Svedberg (unit of sedimentation
	respiratory movement		coefficient)
RMO:	Regional Medical Officer (UK)	s:	second (unit of time)
	Resident Medical Officer (UK)		section
RNA:	ribonucleic acid		singular

	without (Latin *sine*)		streptomycin
	first heart sound		systolic murmur
SA:	sarcoma	SMO:	Senior Medical Officer
	serum albumin	SMON:	subacute myelo-optico-neuro-
	surface area		pathy
S&A:	sugar and acetone	SMR:	submucuous resection
SAE:	stamped addressed envelope	SN:	serum neutralization
SAH:	subarachnoid hemorrhage		student nurse (UK)
Sal:	Salmonella		subnormal
sal:	salicylate	sn:	Snellen test type
Salm:	Salmonella	SNS:	sympathetic nervous system
SAN:	sinoatrial node	SOB:	shortness of breath
sanit:	sanitary	SOBOE:	short of breath on exertion
	sanitation	SOP:	standard operating procedure
sapon:	saponification		surgical outpatients
SAS:	sterile aqueous suspension	SOR:	stimulus-organism-response
sat:	satisfactory	SOS:	supplementary ophthalmic
SB:	shortness of breath		service
	stillbirth	SP:	sacrum to pubis
	Stanford-Binet (intelligence test)		suprapubic
SBE:	shortness of breath on exertion	Sp:	spine
	subacute bacterial endocarditis	sp cd:	spinal cord
SBR:	strict bed rest	sp gr:	specific gravity
SC:	closure of semilunar valves	sph:	spherical
	sacrococcygeal	spir:	spiral
	sick call	spis:	dried (Latin *spissus*)
	subcutaneous	spt:	spirit
	sugar coated		sputum
SCI:	Science Citation Index	SPP:	suprapubic prostatectomy
SCL:	scleroderma	S(R):	single dose
Scler:	sclerosis	SRN:	State Registered Nurse (UK)
SEN:	State Enrolled Nurse (UK)	SQ:	subcutaneous
SG:	Sachs-Georgi (test) (*Also* S-Gt)	ST:	sanitary towel
	specific gravity	st:	stone (weight)
SH:	serum hepatitis	Staph:	Staphylococcus
	sulphydryl	stat:	statistics
	surgical history	stb:	stillborn
sh:	short	sub:	subsequent dose
	shoulder	subq:	subcutaneous
S&H:	speech and hearing	Sulpha:	sulphonamide
SHBG:	sex hormone - binding globulin	sup cit:	cited above (Latin *supra citato*)
SHO:	Senior House Officer (UK)	STS:	serum test for syphilis
SI:	sacroiliac	SU:	sensation unit
	saline injection (abortion)		strontium unit
	saturation index	SV:	sarcoma virus
	soluble insulin	SVC:	superior vena cava
	statutory instrument	SVD:	simple vertex delivery
Sig:	sigmoidoscopy	SVI:	stroke volume index
sig:	label, write (Latin *signa*)	SW:	social worker
sing:	singular (one)	SWD:	short wave diathermy
SL:	small lymphocytes	Sx:	symptom(s)
	streptolysin	syph:	syphilis
	sublingual	syst m:	systolic murmur
SM:	simple mastectomy	sz:	seizure

T:	temperature	tchg:	teaching
	temporary	TCI:	to come in (to hospital)
	term	TCV:	thoracic cage volume
	topical	TD:	tetanus and diphtheria
	transverse		to deliver
	treatment		treatment discontinued
	type		typhoid dysentery
t:	temporal	temp:	temperature
	three times (Latin *ter*)		temporary
	time	TEN:	total excretory nitrogen
T_4:	thyroxine	Tet:	tetanus
TA:	teaching assistant		tetracycline
	temperature, axillary	Tet Vac:	tetanus toxoid
	toxin-antitoxin	ThV:	thoracic vertebra
	triple antigen	TI:	tricuspid incompetence
	tuberculin, alkaline	TIA:	transient ischemic attack
T&A:	tonsillectomy and adenoidec-	tid:	three times daily (Latin *ter in*
	tomy		*die*)
	tonsils and adenoids	TIF:	tumor inducing factor
TAB:	typhoid, paratyphoid A, and	tinct:	tincture
	paratyphoid B (vaccine)	TIP:	translation inhibiting protein
tab:	tablet	TL:	total lipids
TABC:	typhoid, paratyphoid A, para-	T-L:	thymus-dependent lymphocyte
	typhoid B, and paratyphoid C	TLC:	tender loving care
	(vaccine)		total lung capacity
TABT:	combined TAB and tetanus	TLD:	thoracic lymph duct
	toxoid (vaccine)	TMJ:	temporomandibular joint
TABTD:	combined TABT and diphtheria	TN:	temperature normal
	toxoid (vaccine)		true negative
TAF:	toxoid-antitoxin floccules	Tng:	training
	tumor angiogenesis factor	TNV:	tobacco necrosis virus
TAH:	total abdominal hysterectomy	TP:	temperature and pressure
tan:	tangent		threshold potential
TB:	total base		total protein
	tracheal bronchiolar (region)		true positive
	tuberculosis	TPB:	tryptone phosphate broth
TBGP:	total blood granulocyte pod	TPI:	Treponema pallidum immobiliza-
TBI:	total-body irradiation		tion (test)
TBM:	tuberculous meningitis	TPR:	temperature, pulse, respiration
TBP:	testosterone-binding protein		total peripheral resistance
	thyroxine-binding protein	TPT:	total protein tuberculin
tbs:	tablespoon	TPV:	triple polio vaccine
tbsp:	tablespoon	TR:	rectal temperature
TBW:	total body water		temporary resident
	total body weight		therapeutic radiology
TC:	tetracycline (antibiotic)		turbidity reducing
	thermal conductivity	tr:	tincture
	tissue culture		trace
	total cholesterol	trach:	trachea
	type and crossmatch		tracheostomy
TCA_3:	to come again in three days'		tracheotomy
	time	TS:	test solution
TCD:	tissue culture dose		tricuspid stenosis

TS:	triple strength		ux:	wife (Latin *uxor*)
	tubular (tracheal) sound			
T/S:	thyroid/serum (ratio of		V:	vaccinated
	radioiodine)			valve
TSA:	tumor specific antigen			velocity
TSD:	target – skin distance (X-ray)			visit
T-set:	tracheotomy set			visual acuity
TT:	tablet triturate			volume
	tetanus toxoid		v:	against (Latin *versus*)
	transit time (of blood)			very
	tuberculin tested		V7:	visit in 7 days
TTC:	triphenyltetrazolium chloride		vacc:	vaccination
TUD:	total urethral discharge		vag:	vagina
TUR:	transurethral resection		VAH:	virilizing adrenal hyperplasia
Turp:	turpentine		var:	variation
TV:	total volume		VC:	color vision
	transvestite			vital capacity
	Trichomonas vaginalis		VCC:	vasoconstrictor center
	tuberculin volutin		VCG:	vectorcardiogram
Tx:	treatment		VD:	venereal disease
typ:	typical			virus diarrhea
			VDH:	valvular disease of the heart
U:	unerupted (dentistry)		VDM:	vasodepressor material
	unit		VDRL:	Venereal Disease Research
	uracil			Laboratory (test for syphilis)
	urology		VDRT:	venereal disease reference test
235U:	radioactive uranium		VDS:	vasodilator substance
UA:	urinalysis			venereal disease – syphilis
UAE:	unilateral absence of excretion		VE:	vaginal examination
UC:	urinary catheter			varicose eczema
UCL:	urea clearance (test)			ventilation
U & E:	urea and electrolytes			visual efficiency
UD:	ulnar deviation		Vet:	veteran
	urethral discharge			veterinary
UFA:	unesterified fatty acids		VF:	ventricular fibrillation
UG:	urogenital			visual field
UGI:	upper gastrointestinal		VGH:	very good health
UGS:	urogenital system		VI:	vaginal irrigation
UGT:	urogenital tract			*virgo intacta* (Latin)
UHF:	ultrahigh frequency			volume index
UM:	unmarried		VIA:	virus inactivating agent
	upper motor (neuron)		vib:	vibration
UMNL:	upper motor neuron lesion		VP:	vapor pressure
UP:	urinary output			venous pressure
UR:	upper respiratory		VSD:	ventricular septal defect
Ur:	urine		vsn:	vision
ur an:	urine analysis		VSS:	vital signs stable
URI:	upper respiratory infection		V & T:	volume and tension (of pulse)
urogen:	urogenital		VU:	varicose ulcer
URT:	upper respiratory tract			very urgent
USP:	United States Pharmacopeia		VV:	vulva and vagina
USR:	unheated serum reagin (test)			varicose veins
UT:	urinary tract		VW:	vessel wall
UV:	ultraviolet		Vx:	vertex

VZ:	varicella zoster	WxP:	wax pattern
		X:	extra
W:	water		a female chromosome
	weekly dose		times (multiplication sign)
	weight	XES:	X-ray energy spectrometry
	white	X-factor: heme	
	widower	X-matching: cross matching	
	width	Xn:	Christian
w:	watt	XR:	X-ray
	week	XU:	excretory urogram
	wife	XX:	normal female chromosome
WA:	when awake		type
WARF:	Warfarin (a rodenticide)	XY:	normal male chromosome type
Wass:	Wasserman (reaction)	Xyl:	xylose
WB:	water bottle		
	whole blood	Y:	yellow
WBC:	white blood cell		young
	white blood cell count	YCB:	yeast carbon base
WC:	water closet (= toilet)	yd:	yard
	whooping cough	YE:	yellow enzyme
Wd:	ward	y/o:	years old
wds:	wounds	YOB:	year of birth
WDWN: well developed, well nourished		yr:	year
W/F:	white female	ys:	yellow spot
WHO:	World Health Organization		
whp:	whirlpool	Z:	atomic number (symbol)
W/M:	white male		standard score (statistic)
WNL:	within normal limits		zero
WO:	wash out		zone
w/o:	without	ZA:	Zondek-Aschheim
WPW:	Wolff-Parkinson-White	ZE:	Zollinger-Ellison (syndrome)
	(syndrome)	ZN:	Ziehl-Neelsen
WR:	Wassermann reaction	Zn:	zinc
WRC:	washed red cells	Zool:	zoology
WSB:	water soluble base	ZPG:	zero population growth
wt:	weight	ZPO:	zinc peroxide

Surgical and Medical Equipment

Scissors

Dissecting Forceps

Sterilizer Forceps

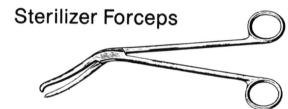

Artery Forceps

Needle Holder

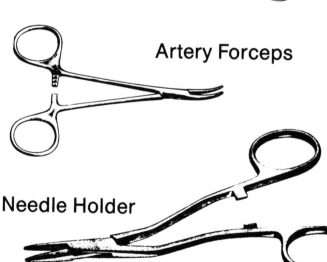

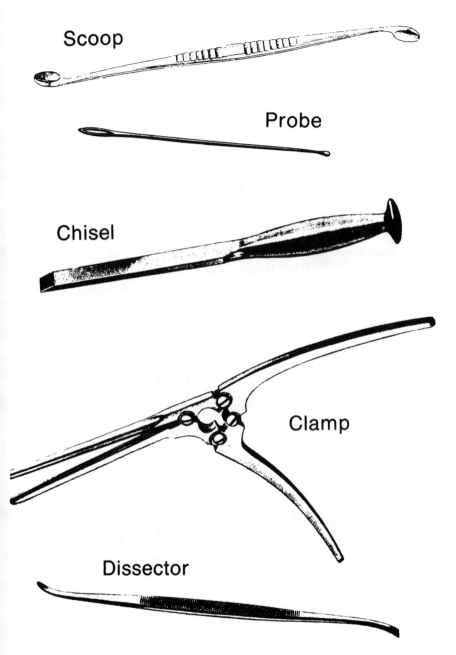

Scoop

Probe

Chisel

Clamp

Dissector

Gouge

Knife

Osteotome

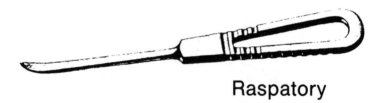

Raspatory

Rugine

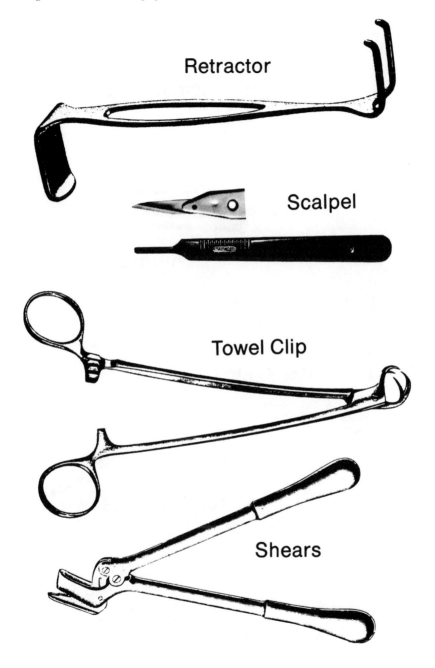

Retractor

Scalpel

Towel Clip

Shears

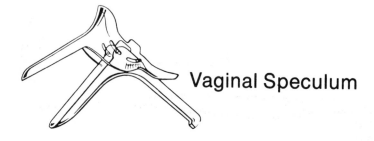

Vaginal Speculum

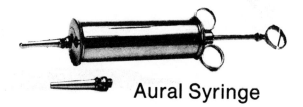

Aural Syringe

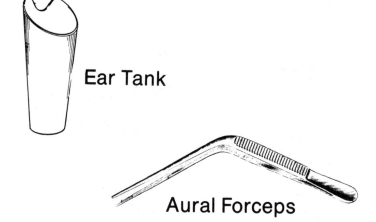

Ear Tank

Aural Forceps

Laryngeal Mirror

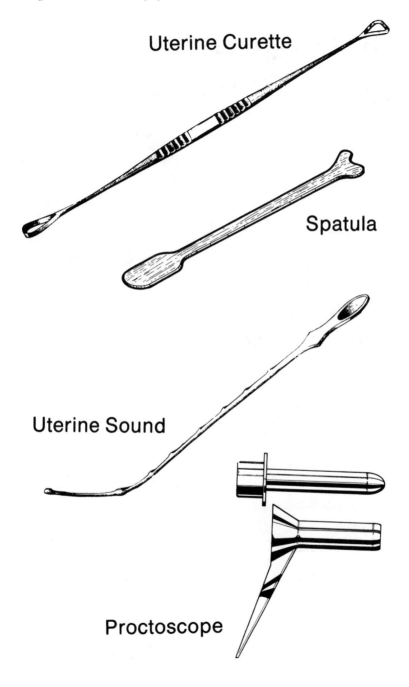

Uterine Curette

Spatula

Uterine Sound

Proctoscope

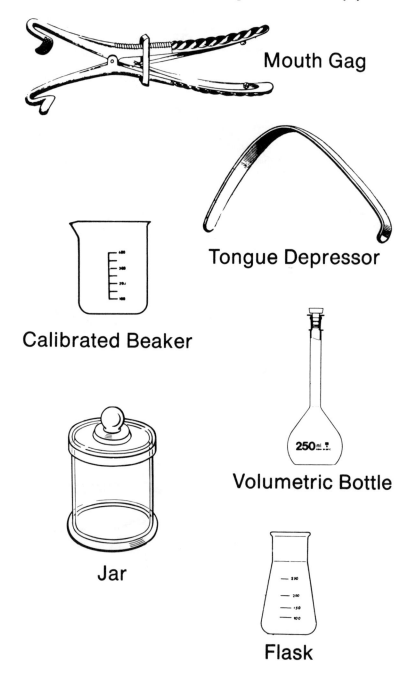

Mouth Gag

Tongue Depressor

Calibrated Beaker

Volumetric Bottle

Jar

Flask

Urine Specimen Glasses

Measuring Cylinder

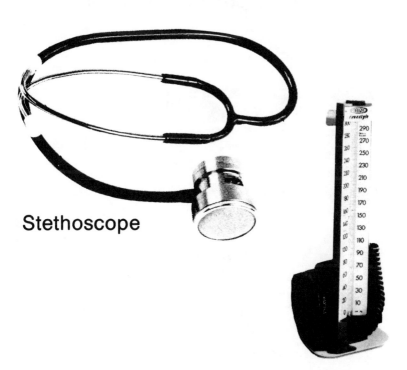

Stethoscope

Sphygmomanometer

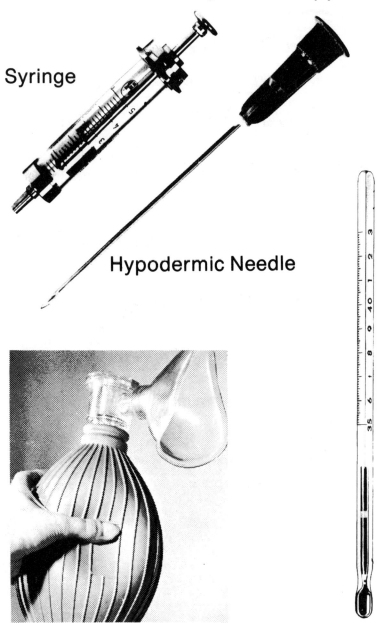

Syringe

Hypodermic Needle

Resuscitator

Thermometer

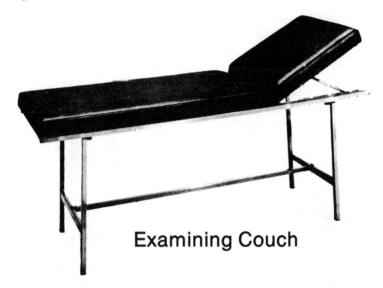

Examining Couch

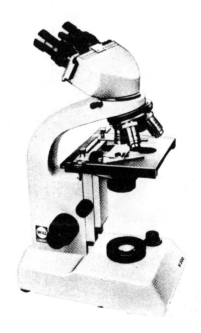

Laboratory Microscope

Surgical and Medical Equipment

Weight Scale

Eye Test Chart

Trolley

English Language Examinations

The examinations in English as a foreign language described here are specifically designed for nonnative speakers. They are basically of two types:

1. General English examinations, which are used to provide test scores for nonnative speakers seeking admission to universities and colleges (e.g., TOEFL, Cambridge Proficiency), and

2. Specific purpose examinations to assess whether professionals are competent to take up a medical appointment in an English-speaking country (e.g., PLAB, ECFMG).

GENERAL ENGLISH EXAMINATIONS
TOEFL (Test of English as a Foreign Language)

Educational Testing Service
TOEFL, PO Box 899
Princeton, NJ 08541
USA
Tel. (609) 921-9000

The purpose of TOEFL is to test the English proficiency of students wishing to be admitted to colleges and universities in the United States and Canada. The test is divided into three sections:

1. Listening Comprehension, parts A, B, C
Listening to a tape recording in Standard American English
2. Structure and Written Expression, parts A, B
Testing your understanding of grammar, syntax, and the structure of written English
3. Reading Comprehension and Vocabulary, parts A, B
Testing the ability to understand academic reading material and the use of words and idiomatic phrases

The tests last about three hours, including time for admission procedures.

TOEFL is given at centers designated by the Educational Testing Service in 135 countries around the world and is administered once a month, 12 times a year.

The *TOEFL Bulletin of Information,* for use by applicants registering for the test, is available at most United States embassies and consulates. A *Handbook for Examinees* and the booklet *Testing American Style* are sent to all those who have registered. *Understanding TOEFL: Test Kit 1, TOEFL Sample Test,* and *Test and Score Manual* can be obtained by writing directly to the Educational Testing Service.

JMB Test in English (Overseas)

The Joint Matriculation Board (JMB)
Manchester M15 6EU
UK
Tel. (061) 273 2565

This test, roughly equivalent to the Cambridge Proficiency, is an advanced level examination for applicants to British universities and colleges.

Paper 1: *Written English*
Three sections: connected writing, individual grammatical and vocabulary items, and reading comprehension

Paper 2: *Aural Comprehension*
Candidates hear two spoken texts and are then asked to complete certain tasks relating to the content of the text

The examination is administered twice yearly in March and June at registered JMB examination centers.

ELTS (English Language Testing Service)

The British Council
10 Spring Gardens
London SW1A 2BN
UK
Tel. (071) 930 8466

and

University of Cambridge Local Examinations Syndicate
Syndicate Buildings
1 Hills Road
Cambridge CB1 2EU
UK
Tel. (0223) 61111

The ELTS test assesses the English language ability of candidates for admission to British or other English-medium educational institutions. Doctors or medical students taking ELTS will normally choose the "Medicine Module" from among the various fields of study covered by the test.

Certificate of Proficiency in English

University of Cambridge Local Examinations Syndicate
Syndicate Buildings
1 Hill Road
Cambridge CB1 2EU
UK
Tel. (0223) 61111

The Cambridge proficiency examination is an advanced level test of general English proficiency. It is an entrance or matriculation requirement for British universities and educational institutions. The examination tests all language skills and consists of 5 papers:

Paper 1: *Reading Comprehension*
A multiple-choice test divided into Section A and Section B to test vocabulary and grammar
Paper 2: *Composition*
Two compositions to be written from a selection of topics
Paper 3: *Use of English*
Sections A and B involve answering questions on a passage and explaining phrases
Paper 4: *Listening Comprehension*
Mainly multiple-choice questions on various recorded texts such as news bulletins, announcements, etc.
Paper 5: *Interview*
Three parts: talking about a photo, reading aloud, and discussion

The examination is administered at recognized centers and is held in June and December. Last dates for entry are 23 March for June and 9 October for December. (Dates are earlier for centers outside the UK.)

MEDICAL ENGLISH EXAMINATIONS
The ECFMG Examination

Educational Commission for Foreign Medical Graduates
3624 Market Street
Philadelphia
Pennsylvania 19104–2685
USA

Foreign medical school graduates must be certified by ECFMG in order to be eligible for appointment to a graduate medical education program in the United States. ECFMG is required for work in hospitals where this involves responsibility for patients. There are some exemptions, such as appointments in pure laboratory research.

The ECFMG examination is in two parts: ECFMG Medicine Examination and ECFMG English Test. The medical portion of the examination includes 420 multiple-choice type questions in English. Most questions are chosen from the clinical fields of surgery, internal medicine, obstetrics and gynecology, mental diseases, and pediatrics. A small number of questions (about one-fourth) are taken from the basic medical sciences of anatomy, behavioral science, biochemistry, microbiology, physiology, pathology, and pharmacology.

The ECFMG English test consists of three parts: comprehension of spoken English, vocabulary, and English structure. All questions are of the multiple-choice type. This English test must be taken as part of the entire ECFMG test. However, if applicants pass the medical portion but fail the English test they will be given the opportunity to retake either the ECFMG English test or the entire ECFMG examination (see above).

The ECFMG examination is given twice yearly in January and July in approved centers around the world. The examination lasts approximately 10 hours and is given on one day.

The PLAB Test

The General Medical Council
Professional and Linguistic Assessments Board
153 Cleveland Street
London WIP 6DE
UK
Tel. (01) 387 2556

This test must be taken by doctors from overseas before they can begin their first appointment in the United Kingdom. It is a test of medical knowledge and competence and of proficiency in English. Candidates must pass both components (medicine and English language) in order to obtain limited registration as medical practitioners in Britain. There are certain exemptions in some circumstances. Enquiries about exemptions should be directed to the General Medical Council.

The complete test consists of six parts, three medical and three linguistic:

Language Component
(a) Comprehension of spoken English paper
(b) Written English paper
(c) Part of the oral examination

Medical Component
(d) Multiple choice paper
(e) Short answers paper
(f) Part of the oral examination

The oral examination lasts 20 minutes and is conducted by two medical examiners. Its purpose is to assess a candidate's proficiency in English and also the capacity to form sensible clinical judgements. One of the two examiners questions the candidates on clinical matters in the first ten minutes, while a colleague listens and assesses the candidate's proficiency in English. During the second 10 minutes the examiners change roles. The examiners' questions will range over the major branches of medicine, and the candidate may be questioned on visual material, such as X-ray films, laboratory reports, or electrocardiograms.

Tests are normally held at least once a month, except in August, at six centers: three in London, two in Edinburgh, and one in Glasgow.

Changes may occur in the exam format or content, and the candidate is strongly advised to seek up-to-date information from the GMC (address above). An explanatory booklet, *Advice to Candidates*, about the PLAB examination is also available from the GMC.

Registration Authorities in the European Community: Addresses

A doctor who has obtained basic qualifications in a member state of the European Economic Community is entitled to practice medicine in any of these countries. Below is a list of the registration authorities in member states.

Belgium
Ordre des Médecins
Place de Jamblinne de Meaux 32
B-1040 Bruxelles

Denmark
National Board of Health
Sundhedsstyrelsen
St. Kongesgade 1
DK-2100 Kobenhavn

France
Conseil National de l'orde des Médecins
60 Boulevard de Latour Maubourg
F-75340 Paris Cedex 07

Department Registration of the Medical Diploma
Prefecture of Police
Health Board
11 Rue des Oursins
75007 Paris

and

Clerk to the Court of First Instance
Palais de Justice
4 Boulevard du Palais
75001 Paris

German Federal Republic
Baden Wurttemberg
Ministerium für Arbeit, Gesundheit
und Sozialordnung
7 Stuttgart 1
Rotebuhlplatz 30
Postfach 1250

Ireland
National Registration Health Authority
The Medical Council
6 Kildare Street
IRL-Dublin 2

Italy
Federazione Nazionale degli Ordini
dei Medici (FNDODM)
Piazza Cola di Rienzo 80/A
1-00192

Luxembourg
National Registration Health Authority
Ministère de la Santé Publique
57 Boulevard de la Petrusse
L-Luxembourg-ville

Netherlands
National Health Authority
De Geneeskundige Hoofdinspecteur van
de Volksgezondheid
Dr. Reijersstraat 10
NL-2265 BA Leidschendam

United Kingdom
National Registration Health Authority
General Medical Council
44 Hallam Street
GB-London W1N 6AE

Professional Organizations: Addresses

IN BRITAIN

British Medical Association
BMA House
Tavistock Square
London WC1H 9JP

British Postgraduate
 Medical Federation
33 Millman Street
London WC1N 3EJ

Council for Postgraduate
 Medical Education in
 England and Wales
7 Marylebone Road
Park Crescent
London NW1 5HA

Department of Health and Social Security
Alexander Fleming House
Newington Causeway
Elephant and Castle
London SE1 6BY

Fellowship of Postgraduate Medicine
Chandos House
1 Queen Anne Street
London W1M 9LE

General Medical Council
44 Hallam Street
London W1N 6AE

General Medical Council
Overseas Registration Division
153 Cleveland Street
London W1P 6DE

General Nursing Council for Scotland
5 Darnaway Street
Edinburgh EH3 6DP

Overseas Doctors' Association
 in the UK Ltd
1 St Peter's Square
Manchester M2 3DN

General Practice Finance Corporation
Tavistock House North
Tavistock Square
London WC1H 9JL

Medical Defence Union
3 Devonshire Place
London W1N 2EA

Medical & Dental Union of Scotland
105 St Vincent Street
Glasgow G2

Medical Insurance Agency
BMA House
Tavistock Square
London WC1H 9JD

Medical Practitioners' Union
79 Camden Road
London NW1 9ES

Medical Protection Society
50 Hallam Street
London W1N 6DE

Medical Research Council
20 Park Crescent
London W1N 4AL

National Advice Centre
The Medical Adviser
Council for Postgraduate Medical
  Education
7 Marylebone Road
London NW1 5HH

Worshipful Society of
  Apothecaries of London
Apothecaries Hall
Black Friars Lane
London EC4 6EJ

Royal Societies and Colleges In Britain

Royal College of General Practitioners
14 Princes Gate
Hyde Park
London SW7 1PU

Royal College of Obstetricians and
  Gynaecologists
27 Sussex Place
Regents Park
London NW1 4RG

Royal College of Pathologists
2 Carlton House Terrace
London SW1Y 5AF

Royal College of Physicians, Edinburgh
9 Queen Street
Edinburgh EH2 1JQ

Royal College of Physicians of London
11 St. Andrew's Place
Regents Park
London NW1 4LE

Royal College of Physicians & Surgeons
  of Glasgow
242 St Vincent Street
Glasgow G2

Royal College of Psychiatrists
17 Belgrave Square
London WS1X 8PG

Royal College of Midwives
15 Mansfield Street
London W1M 0BE

Royal College of Radiologists
28 Portland Place
London W1N 4DE

Royal College of Surgeons of Edinburgh
18 Nicolson Street
Edinburgh EH8 9DW

Royal College of Surgeons in Ireland
St Stephen's Green
Dublin 2

Royal College of Surgeons of England
Lincoln's Inn Fields
London WC2A 3PN

Royal Institute of Public Health and
  Hygiene
28 Portland Place
London W1N 4DE

Royal Medical Society
Student's Centre
Bristo Square
Edinburgh EH8 9AL

Royal Society of Medicine
1 Wimpole Street
LondonW1M 8AE

Royal Society of Tropical Medicine &
  Hygiene
26 Portland Place
London W1N 4EY

PROFESSIONAL ORGANIZATIONS IN THE USA

Aerospace Medical Association
Washington National Airport
Washington, DC 20001

American Academy of Allergy and
  Immunology
611 East Wells Street
Milwaukee, WI 53202

American Academy of Family Physicians
1740 West 92nd Street
Kansas City, MO 64114

American Academy of Ophthalmology
1833 Fillmore Street
POB 7424
San Francisco, CA 94120

American Academy of Otolaryngology
Suite 302
1101 Vermont Avenue, NW
Washington, DC 20005

American Academy of Pediatrics
141 Northwest Point Blvd
POB 927
Elk Grove Village, IL 60007

American Academy of Periodontology
211 East Chicago Avenue
Chicago, IL 60611

American Association of Anatomists
Department of Anatomy
Medical College of Virginia
Richmond, VA 23298

American Association of Immunologists
9650 Rockville Pike
Bethesda, MD 20814

American Association of Pathologists
9650 Rockville Pike
Bethesda, MD 20814

American Cancer Society Inc.
90 Park Avenue
New York, NY 10016

American College of Obstetricians and
  Gynecologists
600 Maryland, SW
Suite 300
Washington, DC 20024

American College of Physicians
4200 Pine Street
Philadelphia, PA 19104

American College of Surgeons
55 East Erie Street
Chicago, IL 60611

American Dental Association
211 East Chicago Avenue
Chicago, IL 60611

American Dietetic Association
430 North Michigan Avenue
Chicago, IL 60611

American Geriatrics Society
770 Lexington Avenue
Suite 400
New York, NY 10021

American Gynecological and Obstetrical
  Society
Magee Women's Hospital
Pittsburgh, PA 15213

American Heart Association
7320 Greenville Avenue
Dallas, TX 75231

American Hospital Association
840 North Lake Shore Drive
Chicago, IL 60611

American Institute of Nutrition
9650 Rockville Pike
Bethesda, MD 20814

American Laryngological Rhinological and
  Otological Society Inc.
POB 155
East Greenville, PA 18041

American Lung Association
1740 Broadway
New York, NY 10019-4374

American Medical Association
535 North Dearborn Street
Chicago, IL 60610

American Medical Technologists
710 Higgins Road
Park Ridge, IL 60068

American Medical Women's Association
465 Grand Sreet
New York, NY 10002

American Neurological Association
Administrative Office
POB 14730
Minneapolis, MN 55414

American Occupational Therapy
    Association
1383 Piccard Drive
Rockville, MD 20850

American Optometric Association
243 N. Lindbergh Boulevard
St. Louis, MO 63141

American Pediatric Society
POB 14871
St. Louis, MO 63178

American Physical Therapy Association
111 N. Fairfax Street
Alexandria, VA 22314

American Physiological Society
9650 Rockville Pike
Bethesda, MD 20814

American Psychiatric Association
1400 K Street, NW
Washington, DC 20005

American Public Health Association
1015 15th Street, NW
Washington, DC 20005

American Rheumatism Association
1314 Spring Street, NW
Atlanta, GA 30309

American Roentgen Ray Society
1891 Preston White Drive
Reston, VA 22091

American Society for Clinical Investigation
Department of Medicine
College of Physicians and Surgeons
Columbia University
630 West 168th Street
New York, NY 10032

American Society for Medical Technology
330 Meadowfern Drive
Houston, TX 58004

American Society for Microbiology
1913 I Street NW
Washington, DC 20006

American Society for Pharmacology and
    Experimental Therapeutics Inc.
9650 Rockville Pike
Bethesda, MD 20814

American Society of Clinical Hypnosis
2250 East Devon Avenue
Suite 336
Des Plaines, IL 60018

American Society of Clinical Pathologists
2100 West Harrison Street
Chicago, IL 60612

American Society of Human Genetics
Executive Office
15501-B Monons Drive
Derwood, MD 20855

American Society of Tropical Medicine
    and Hygiene
POB 29837
San Antonio, TX 78229

American Speech-Language-Hearing
    Association
10801 Rockville Pike
Rockville, MD 20852

American Surgical Association
Department of Surgery
Massachusetts General Hospital
32 Fruit Street
Boston, MA 02114

American Urological Association Inc.
1120 North Charles Street
Baltimore, MD 21201

Association of American Medical Colleges
Suite 200
One Dupont Circle NW
Washington, DC 20036

Association of American Physicians
University of Texas
Southwestern Medical School
5323 Harry Hines Blvd.
Dallas, TX 75235

Center for the Study of Aging and Human
  Development
Duke University
Durham, NC 27710

Medical Society of the State of New York
420 Lakeville Road
Lake Success, NY 11042

National Mental Health Association
1-21 Prince Street
Alexandria, VA 22314-2971

National Society for Medical Research
Suite 700
1029 Vermont Avenue NW
Washington, DC 20005

New York Academy of Medicine
East 103rd Street
New York, NY 10029

Radiological Society of North America
1415 W. 22nd Street
Oak Brook, IL 60521

Society of Medical Jurisprudence
400 Park Avenue
New York, NY 10022

Southern Medical Association
35 Lakeshore Drive
PO Box 63656
Birmingham, AL 35219-0088

ROYAL COLLEGES AND PROFESSIONAL ORGANIZATIONS IN CANADA

Academy of Medicine
288 Bloor Street
West Toronto
M5S 1V8

Canadian Association of Anatomists
Department of Anatomy & Cell Biology
University of Alberta
Edmonton
Alta T6G 2H7

Canadian Association of Optometrists
Suite 207
77 Metcalfe Street
Ottawa
Ontario KIP 5L6

Canadian Dental Association
1815 Alta Vista Drive
Ottawa
Ontario KIG 3Y6

Canadian Lung Association
75 Albert Street
Suite 908
Ottawa
Ontario KIP

Canadian Medical Association
POB 8650
Ottawa
Ontario K1G OG8

Canadian Paediatric Society
Children's Hospital of Eastern Ontario
401 Smyth Road
Ottawa
Ontario K1H 8L1

Canadian Pharmaceutical Association
1785 Alta Vista Drive
Ottawa
Ontario K1G 3Y6

Canadian Physiological Society
Dept. of Medical Physiology
University of Calgary
Calgary

Canadian Psychiatric Association
225 Lisgar St.
Suite 103
Ottawa
Ontario K2P OC6

Canadian Public Health Association
1335 Carling Avenue
Suite 210
Ottawa
Ontario K1Z 8N8

Canadian Society for Nutritional Sciences
Department of Nutrition
Montreal University
Montreal
Que H3C 3S7

Pharmacological Society of Canada
Faculty of Pharmaceutical Sciences
University of British Columbia
Vancouver BC V6T 1W5

Royal College of Physicians and Surgeons
   of Canada
74 Stanley
Ottawa
Ontario K1M 1P4

Society of Obstetricians and Gynaecologists
   of Canada
Suite 210
!4 Prince Arthur Avenue
Toronto
Ontario M5R 1A9

ROYAL COLLEGES AND PROFESSIONAL
ORGANIZATIONS IN AUSTRALIA

Australasian College of Dermatologists
271 Bridge Road
Glebe
NSW 2037

Australian and New Zealand Society of
  Nuclear Medicine
c/o The Science Centre
35-42 Clarence Street
Sydney
NSW 2000

Australian Association of Clinical
  Biochemists
Department of Biochemistry
Royal Perth Hospital
GPO Box X2213
Perth
WA 6001

Australian Association of Neurologists
Department of Clinical Neurophysiology
Alfred Hospital
Commercial Road
Prahran
Vic. 3181

Australian Dental Association
116 Pacino Highway
North Sydney
POB 411
NSW 2060

Australian Institute of Homoeopathy
P.O. Box 122
Roseville
NSW 2069

Australian Medical Association
Box 20
Glebe
NSW 2037

Australian Optometrical Association
Box 185
Carlton South
Vic. 3053

Australian Physiological and Pharmaco-
  logical Society
Department of Physiology and Pharma-
  cology
University of Sydney
NSW 2006

Australian Physiotherapy Association
POB 119
Concord
NSW 2137

College of Nursing, Australia
Suite 22
431 St Kilda Road
Melbourne
Vic. 3004

Medical Foundation
Coppleson Institute
University of Sydney
Sydney
NSW 2906

Royal Australasian College of Dental
  Surgeons
64 Castlereagh Street
Sydney
NSW 2000

Royal Australasian College of Physicians
145 Macquarie Street
Sydney
NSW

Royal Australasian College of Radiologists
37 Lower Fort Street
Millers Point
NSW 2000

Royal Australasian College of Surgeons
Spring Street
Melbourne
Vic. 3000

Royal Australian College of Ophthalmo-
  logists
27 Commonwealth Street
Sydney
NSW 2010

Royal College of Pathologists of Australasia
Durham Hall
207 Albion Street
Surry Hills
NSW 2010